THEY SHALL
FIGHT
AGAINST THEE

VALENTIN NTCHA

Order this book online at www.trafford.com
or email orders@trafford.com

Most Trafford titles are also available at major online book retailers.

Unless otherwise stated, Bible texts are from the King James Version.

Printed in the United States of America.

ISBN: 978-1-4907-0876-8 (sc)
ISBN: 978-1-4907-0877-5 (hc)
ISBN: 978-1-4907-0878-2 (e)

Library of Congress Control Number: 2013912834

Trafford rev. 08/21/2013

 www.trafford.com

North America & international
toll-free: 1 888 232 4444 (USA & Canada)
fax: 812 355 4082

But rise, and stand upon thy feet:
for I have appeared unto thee for this purpose,
to make thee a minister and a witness
both of these things which thou hast seen,
and of those things in the which I will appear unto thee;
Delivering thee from the people
and from the Gentiles,
unto whom now I send thee,
To open their eyes,
and to turn them from darkness to light,
and from the power of Satan unto God,
that they may receive forgiveness of sins,
and inheritance among them
which are sanctified by faith that is in me.

—Acts of the Apostles 26:16-18

CONTENTS

LIST OF TABLES

FOREWORD

This manual is titled *They Shall Fight against Thee.* Our enemies are at war against us and are eager to destroy us. The devil rose up against God's creation. This wicked serpent knows he has little time, and he does not want to go alone to perdition. He wants to bring as many people as possible with him. However, many who are committed to follow the Lord devoutly fall into all sorts of snares and tricks from the enemy.

As a result, my husband wrote this book to open the eyes of the multitude on the realities of the world of darkness, to arm ourselves with knowledge and prayers to counteract the arrows of the enemy, to increase our discernment on activities of everyday life where the devil tries to ensnare us, and to free ourselves from its clutches.

However, before you continue to read this book, before these prayers become helpful to you, give your life to Jesus Christ. Pray like this:

> *Lord Jesus Christ, I acknowledge that I am a sinner. I need you. Come into my life. Be my Lord and Savior. I renounce Satan, his demons, and his tactics. Holy*

Spirit, come live within me, come to teach me and comfort me. In the name of Jesus I pray.

I seal your prayer in the precious blood of Jesus. I pray that his blood covers you and accompanies you during your reading.

Beloved, there is still hope. This Bible passage is proof.

> And they shall fight against thee; but they shall not prevail against thee; for I am with thee, saith the Lord, to deliver thee. (Jeremiah 1:19)

Now that the Lord Jesus is with you, you will have the victory. The Lord of hosts will certainly deliver you. Be blessed.

Your sister in battle,

Yasmine Félix

ACKNOWLEDGMENT

First of all, I bless the Lord, who inspired me through his Word, on the teachings contained in this book. May the honor and glory be given unto him.

I also thank all those whom God has placed on my path, to support and advise me. May the King of kings bless you abundantly.

Finally, this book project became effective mostly because of the great contribution of the one that my heart loves. I sincerely thank my wife, Yasmine, for the work and effort she has provided for the success of this book. May the grace of God, which surpasses all understanding, dwell with you.

INTRODUCTION

In this manual for spiritual warfare, the Lord, our God, exhibits the works of the enemy. In addition, he reveals his tricks and manipulations. The times are evil. Only prayer will enable us to have victory.

> Call unto me, and I will answer thee, and show thee great and mighty things, which thou knowest not. (Jeremiah 33:3)

In the past, you may not have discerned some spiritual activities that you saw. The enemy has used your ignorance to hurt you. Beloved, now God reveals these activities that they may no longer be a mystery for you. You have invoked God in fasting and prayer. You've sought his face during retreats or conventions. Your God wants to answer you this time around. In order to obtain his answer, he wants you to pay attention to him. The book of Joshua says,

> This book of the law shall not depart out of thy mouth; but thou shalt meditate therein day and night, that thou mayest observe to do according to all that is written therein: for then thou shalt make

thy way prosperous, and then thou shalt have good
success. (Joshua 1:8)

For success in the spiritual warfare in which we are engaged, we
must meditate on the Word of God day and night. This Word
provides us profound knowledge, which enables us to put to
flight our most unruly enemies. These will flee without being
pursued; they will tremble at the sound of the wind. Here is
the weapon that the Lord has given us to reduce to naught our
antagonists and their initiatives.

However, if we fail to meditate on these scriptures, it will be
difficult to push back the enemy out of our territory and bring
the battle to his camp. By meditating on the Word of God, our
minds will open up to the projects that are undertaken by our
opponents. Our understanding will cause their raids to fail,
and we will be totally freed from their ambush. Through the
study of this manual, the Lord will take away the strength of
our adversaries. The Lord will destroy their weapons from their
hands.

The love of God surpasses all. He commanded us to love our
neighbor as ourselves. As a Christian committed to spiritual
warfare, our life on earth resembles that of a soldier. We must
fight the good fight of faith. Despite the fact that we walk in the
flesh,[1] we do not war after the *flesh*. The prayers that are found
in this manual are not directed against an individual or a group
of people but only against Satan and his kingdom. May God
help every reader to make good use of it.

---

[1]   At the end of this book, a glossary explains the words put in
italics in the text.

Beware, these prayers should not be read or recited. They must be carried out with aggression so that your mind, your soul, and your body are involved. The model of violent prayers has been demonstrated to us by the Lord Jesus in Luke 22:44: "And being in an agony he prayed more earnestly: and his sweat was as it were great drops of blood falling down to the ground."

Similarly, in Luke 18:13, the Bible tells the story of a publican who prayed in the temple, striking his breast. These two examples reveal patterns of aggressive prayers that took place in the Bible. This demonstrates that warfare prayer began a long time ago.

My advice to the readers of this manual, still novices in the type of warfare prayers, is to anoint themselves with anointing oil before or after each session of prayer. Most likely, spiritual forces will respond to these prayers to intimidate the reader. To obtain anointing oil, get a bottle of olive oil and pray as follows: "I converted this oil into the blood of Jesus, in the mighty name of Jesus."

Beloved, may God keep you, and may he bless the works of your hands.

CHAPTER I

JUDGMENTS OF THE SPIRITUAL WORLD

The purpose of this message, which the Lord gives us through his Word, is to draw our attention to the negative effects of the decisions of the spiritual world in our lives. Beloved, I pray that the Lord opens your precious heart so that you may understand the word of truth. It will bring a major change in your life, in your family, and in your nation. So when you reject the knowledge given to you by God the Creator, you will be equally rejected and even deprived of his priesthood (Hosea 4:6). The teaching is taken from the passage in the book of 1 Kings 22:1-22.

1.1. THE TRUCE

For years, the children of Israel were at war against the Syrians. Then, the two sides decided to suspend their attacks against each other. Each nation withdrew from the battlefield. This time of withdrawal is called a truce and does not mean the end of the war. Sometimes people are continuously pounded by the attacks of Satan or their enemies. To overcome this violence, they pray regularly. One day, they will realize that the conflict has stopped. However, this is not the end. Beloved, the devil may recede due to the resistance that you create through your prayers. However, this cunning snake will rearrange his plans to come back in force.

In total, the truce lasted three years between King Ahab and the Syrians. King Ahab was visited by the King Jehoshaphat, who reigned over Judah. During this meeting, wicked thoughts crossed the mind of King Ahab. This king of Israel decided to break the truce. Because of the territory occupied by the Syrians, who belonged to Israel (1 Kings 22:3), he invited his fellow, the king of Judah, to join him with the intention of going to war against the Syrians. Jehoshaphat replied, "I am as thou art, my people as thy people, my horses as thy horses" (1 Kings 22:4b).

1.2.   THE STRENGTHENING

King Jehoshaphat accepted the offer of the king of Israel to fight alongside him against the Syrians. King Ahab mustered his troops and gathered his government officials and his military leaders to develop plans and strategies of war against his opponents. Now that the king of Judah seconded him, he saw his troops, equipment, and weapons of war grow. King Ahab's heart was filled with joy as he was persuaded to run a strong invasion against Syria. Now the Syrian nation had to fight two enemies: Israel and Judah.

Beloved, let us watch and pray. Satan, the devil, may have gone away from you for a moment. Nevertheless, it is one of his tricks. He reorganizes himself to come back against you with force. In the spiritual world, reinforcement always occurs after an initial setback. Satan is not easily discouraged; he will make other plans, and he will return in force at the appropriate time, as confirmed by the Gospel according to Luke, who says, "He departed from him for a season." (Luke 4:13b)

1.3. CONSULTING SPIRITUAL FORCES

In 1 Kings 22:5, Jehoshaphat declares to the king of Israel, "Enquire, I pray thee, at the word of the Lord to day."

King Jehoshaphat wanted to make sure, first of all, that the war against Syria in which he engaged himself was approved by the God that the children of Israel and the people of Judah served. For this reason, he summoned the prophets in Israel so they can consult their God and thus receive an informed response (1 Kings 22:6). The action of Jehoshaphat demonstrates that people seek spiritual forces for guidance on their projects. Undoubtedly, they come in contact with these forces through crooks, soothsayers, clairvoyants, or even astrologers.

1.4. VISION OF MICAH THE PROPHET

The last *prophet* invited by the king of Israel and the king of Judah was Micah. Four hundred other prophets had come before him. They had already confirmed that God approved of the invasion against Syria. Now, let's consider the vision of the prophet Micah to understand how the judgments of the spiritual world affect the plans of men on this earth:

> And he said, Hear thou therefore the word of the Lord: I saw the Lord sitting on his throne, and all the host of heaven standing by him on his right hand and on his left. And the Lord said, Who shall persuade Ahab, that he may go up and fall at

Ramoth-gilead? And one said on this manner, and another said on that manner. (1 Kings 22:19-20)

Beloved, while Ahab and Jehoshaphat, his visitor, were assembled in the physical world, his government was preparing attack plans against Syria. He was planning the war strategies, reviewing his material, and preparing his troops for an invasion. At the same time, in the spiritual world, in the third heaven, a meeting was held, which purpose was to make decision contrary to that of King Ahab. The spirit world was about to oppose a project developed in the physical world. The God of Israel, who resides in the third heaven, was opposed to the intentions of King Ahab. He had immediately gathered with his *angels* to put an end to the action of Ahab. This action is one of the reasons why many fail when they undertake an activity or when they embark on major projects.

Surprisingly, some people think they have fallen from heaven. Indeed, they forget that they come from a family, and that prior to their birth, lived their fathers, grandfathers, and great-grandfathers. In *turn*, these ancestors served *strange gods*. These *deities* still exist, despite the death of their ancestors. Thus, in the same manner that God has opposed the project of King Ahab, in the spiritual world, these ancestral gods do the same against these individuals.

That being said, we must learn a lesson from what would happen to King Ahab. It is important to know that whenever we elaborate a project, at the same time, in the spiritual world, powers gather to lead us to failure. These powers can be found either in our foundation, in the air, underneath the water, and in other dimensions.

1.5. JUDGMENT AGAINST THE KING IN THE SPIRITUAL WORLD

The decision taken by God and his angels at the meeting in heaven against the plan of King Ahab (1 Kings 22:20) is that the latter would be persuaded, he would go to war, and he would perish on the battlefield.

During this meeting, the discussion was opened to discern the method of seduction to be used against King Ahab. Each of the present angels came before God the Father to expose his method to entice King Ahab. Nevertheless, nothing was selected by God. The example of King Ahab demonstrates how meetings held in the spiritual realm affect human beings' projects that live in the physical world.

Based on this revelation, here's what we can conclude. Projects can be aborted, abandoned due to obstacles or theft. In addition, people who start projects are excluded of their own project, are killed before the end, or have a calamity befall them. Others are abandoned by their partners without cause.

Dear brothers and sisters, whenever you have a project to achieve, whether it be a wedding, a trip, a construction, an investment, or buying a house, and so forth, you must pray to reverse the judgments of the spiritual world erected against what you undertake. Be advised that the devil knows what you're undertaking. The Bible advises us,

> Be sober, be vigilant; because your adversary the
> devil, as a roaring lion, walketh about, seeking whom
> he may devour. (1 Peter 5:8)

1.6. DECISION MANAGEMENT IN THE SPIRITUAL WORLD

The methods proposed by the angels were not convincing before God. However, in 1 Kings 22:21, we read,

> And there came forth a spirit, and stood before the Lord, and said, I will persuade him.

Thereby, the spirit suggested to God his method to entice King Ahab.

This evil spirit took the opportunity to complain of Job (Job 1:6-10). In the spiritual world, nothing is carried out by chance. This universe has an excellent organization. Let us look at the following table with the activities of spirits during a decision making in the spiritual world and the biblical references thereto.

Table 1:   Activities of spirits during decision making in the spiritual world

Activities of the spirits	Biblical references
Choose the weapon or the person to send against their antagonist.	"And the Lord said, Who shall persuade Ahab" (1 Kings 22:20a).
Decide the place of destruction or attack.	"That he may go up and fall at Ramoth-gilead?" (1 Kings 22:20b).
Communicate with each other in the spiritual world.	"And one said on this manner, and another said on that manner" (1 Kings 22:20c).
In the invisible world, select which of them will fulfill the mission decided.	"I will persuade him" (1 Kings 22:21b).

Essentially, the spirit that appeared before God was Satan, the devil. As he did during this meeting, this fallen cherub continues to go before the throne of God to claim souls. During the rally, the Lord issued his will to punish the king of Israel, and this gave a golden opportunity to the old serpent, also present at the meeting, to propose himself to take action against Ahab. Since this idea came from the Lord, he could attack freely King Ahab in such a way that he could not have done without God's consent. The Lord asked him to explain his intentions. According to this context, we can say that in the spiritual world, for a mission to be assigned to a spirit, he must demonstrate to his superiors the effectiveness of his plan.

Note that, when you sin against God and he wants to deliver you into the hands of the devil, that wicked spirit does not directly destroy you. There is a procedure where the Lord must approve the destruction plan of the enemy. Thus, Satan has made a commitment before the Lord and before the angels to accomplish the mission. In return, God tested the seduction technique he would use to see if it would be appropriate before entrusting him with this assignment.

1.7. ELABORATION OF SATAN'S PLAN AGAINST KING AHAB

Here is Satan's seduction against King Ahab, while the enemy presents it to God. In 1 Kings 22:22, the Bible declares,

> And the Lord said unto him, Wherewith? And he said, I will go forth, and I will be a lying spirit in the mouth of all his prophets. And he said, Thou shalt persuade him, and prevail also: go forth, and do so.

As we just read, the technique used by Satan to deceive King Ahab was approved by God, who gave his authorization. Soon afterwards, Satan withdrew. This ancient serpent was going to use cunning lies against the king of Israel. As a matter of fact, Satan is behind every lie, whether big or small. Yet God hates lying, as he said in his Word,

> He that telleth lies shall not tarry in my sight.
> (Psalm 101:7b)

Moreover, when someone is lying, it means that he has an unclean spirit. The devil controls his mouth and will use it against another person. Therefore, he becomes horrible before God. Beloved, the *spirit* of lies affects those who like to manipulate others. Do you know how many people have died or lost their property, their families, their jobs, etc., because they listened to tales? This ancient weapon used by Satan against King Ahab continues to cause havoc today.

In a short time, the lying spirit had controlled four hundred prophets. This epidemic lie had spread throughout the land of Israel. In this end time, the enemy still has the ability to use a single spirit to afflict a village, an environment, or a province of the same disease. In a place where people suffer from the same evil, it is possible that this activity originates from one *demon*. The prophets used a lying spirit and allowed themselves to be manipulated by Satan. They told false prophecies to cause the death of King Ahab. Even today, this type of *false prophets* invades our churches, our media, and our cities. Their prophecies have caused the death of many people. They do not hear the voice of God but rather that of unclean spirits. In conclusion, beloved, the fact that many prophets give you the same revelation does not imply that these prophecies truly come from God. The example of these four hundred prophets is a proof that we must consider or mediated on.

1.8. HOW SATAN SUCCEEDED HIS MISSION ON EARTH

The Lord said, "Thou shalt persuade him, and prevail also: go forth, and do so" (1 Kings 22:22b).

As soon as the devil received permission, Satan left the heavens for the earth to perform his task. Beloved, the spirits in the spiritual world travel. They roam the earth, the sea, the sky, and other areas. For example, they can come from forests or cemeteries to stroll in our environments (Job 1:7). The sentence made in the spiritual realm against King Ahab was to be performed in the physical world. We also note that when a verdict is pronounced in the spiritual world against an individual, then a spirit, an angel, or a demon is sent against the person to enforce the sentence.

To perform the decision of the spiritual realm in the physical world, Satan had to choose those working in collaboration with the king. As a spirit, he needs a physical body to do his work. That is why Satan entered the mouth of the prophets and manifested himself in the form of a spirit of lies and thus brought these prophets to take part in the destruction of the king of Israel.

What lesson can we learn from this action of Satan? In table 2, we will look at the capacity of spirits as well as biblical references for each of these capacities.

Table 2: Capacity of spirits and biblical references

Capacity of spirits	Biblical references
Enter a body	"I will be a lying spirit in the mouth of all his prophets"(1 Kings 22:22b).
Control organs and parts of the human body	"I will be a lying spirit in the mouth" (1 Kings 22:22b).
Know the identity of people	"Of all his prophets" (1 Kings 22:22b).
Subdue people to their will	"Thou shalt persuade him, and prevail also" (1 Kings 22:22c).

Given the foregoing, one spirit can control a group of people to get them to share the same feeling, unite, speak, think, or walk the same way. In the story we just read, the four hundred prophets have all made the same misrepresentation.

In conclusion, beloved, seduction and lying go hand in hand; one is the root of the other. This is how the spiritual world operates. Spirits take decisions in the unseen world to execute them in the physical world. From that moment, the demons manage to penetrate material bodies (humans, animals, objects, etc.) in order to fulfill the judgment. Let us refuse that Satan uses us to destroy our neighbors and our projects by carrying out the following prayers.

1.9. PRAYER SECTION

1. Every power that helps my opponents to fight me, fall in a evil net, in the name of Jesus.
2. I disrupt the powers that regroup in the spirit world to confront me, in the name of Jesus.

3. Any weapon formed against my projects in the spiritual world, be of no effect, in the name of Jesus.

4. I take back my projects from the hands of the forces of darkness, in the name of Jesus.

5. Every spirit in the spiritual world, consulted by those who devise evil against me, fall face toward the ground, in the name of Jesus.

6. I cancel the words of the mouths that prophesy evil against my projects, in the name of Jesus.

7. I overthrow the thrones of the world of darkness around, which debates are held against my projects, in the name of Jesus.

8. Any announcement launched in the unseen world against the fulfillment of my projects, you will not come to pass, in the name of Jesus.

9. Every strange god seated on his throne, contesting my projects on earth, descend and sit down in the dust, in the name of Jesus.

10. During the realization of my project, take away from me, Lord, discouragement, bad luck, sudden death, accidents, doubt, fear, disease, mistakes, confusion, and memory loss programmed by the world of darkness, in the name of Jesus.

11. You, my hands, as you begin the execution of this project, you will complete it, in the name of Jesus.

12. No spirit in the world of darkness will be worthy to stop this project in this land of the living, in the name of Jesus.

13. Every spirit in the spiritual world who vowed to kill me before, during, or after the completion of this project, graze grass like an ox, in the name of Jesus.

14. Every spirit that comes from the waters or from the heavens to the earth in order to enforce judgments against me, I put a heavy yoke on your neck, in the name of Jesus.

15. I divided the languages of the spirits gathered in the spirit world against my activities on earth, in the name of Jesus.

16. I bind the powers that control the mouths of all those who will collaborate with me in this project, in the name of Jesus.

17. I strike of dizziness the spirit who wants to use others to spoil my plans, in the name of Jesus.

18. Lord, by your hurricane, scatter the talks that were held by the spirits under the water, in the air, in the first and second heaven, in the name of Jesus.

19. Let the decisions taken against me by the forces gathered in the spirit world cause them to stumble, in the name of Jesus.

20. By the blood of Jesus, I declare null and void the judgments of the spiritual world on my projects in the physical world, in the name of Jesus.

21. The evil spoken against me by the spirits gathered in the spiritual world will fall back on their heads, in the name of Jesus.

22. The communication of forces in the spiritual realm concerning the affairs of my life will bring forth nothingness, in the name of Jesus.

23. Every spirit that received the mandate to execute decisions against me in the physical world, descend into the horrible pit, in the name of Jesus.

24. I bind the spirit of lying by which men prophesied on my projects, in the name of Jesus.

25. Every prophecy whose mission is to cause death, destruction or failure, be aborted, in the name of Jesus.

26. Every evil power roaming around my plans to devour them, flee without being pursued, in the name of Jesus.

27. Divine powers, watch over my projects, in the name of Jesus.

CHAPTER II

TRAVELING AND ANCESTRAL FORCES

P olitical problems, economic crises, natural disasters, conflicts, and wars have created a migration flow. Thus, people leave their home countries for another in order to improve their living conditions. Unfortunately, some do not progress as they hoped. After many failures, these people ask themselves several questions. Why is there no change in our destiny? What is the cause of this situation? Are we under the influence of a curse? Don't we have college degrees? Only the Lord of hosts will be able to answer their many questions. Let us look in his Word to understand the hidden mysteries of traveling and ancestral forces. The book of Genesis 46:1-7 will serve as our guide.

2.1. JACOB'S JOURNEY FROM HEBRON TO BEER-SHEBA

Jacob moved to Hebron, where he lived, to Beer-sheba, his destination. The Bible says he departed with all that he had (Genesis 46:1). Jacob, called Israel, a name which was given to him by the angel of God, had brought everything. He left nothing to Hebron, not even a needle. Thus do some people who immigrate to a new environment. They bring with them everything that belongs to them. They settle into their new home with their *strange gods*, their evil altars, their religion, their culture, etc.

In light of the foregoing, beloved, if you are hosting people in your home, have the goodwill to know what is in their belongings. Be sure to ask for further information about the content of the affairs of those traveling with you. For example, the cup that Joseph used to predict the future was put in Benjamin's bag, his younger brother, without his knowledge. This cup was a trap for Joseph's brothers. They were accused of being thieves and of having rewarded evil for good (Genesis 44). This is why we need to know the contents of our personal effects when we travel. Eventually, occult objects can be transported from one place to another during expeditions, without our being aware.

In this regard, allow me to tell you a little anecdote. Here is the story of a young African who went into exile in the United States. To regularize his situation in the American territory, he applied for political asylum. He had to pass three times in front of an immigration judge. According to his testimony, this African said that during the first two interviews, the judge in charge of his case was not courteous to him at all. Depressed, he went to see his sister for her to support him in prayer before his last interview. His sister asked him to get rid of everything he possessed that did not honor God. He got rid of the sand he had taken on his father's grave before his trip to the United States. This is how his third interview was successful.

2.2. Jacob offers sacrifices to the God of his father

As for Jacob, he left Hebron to go to Egypt with his family, invited by Pharaoh. When he arrived to Beer-sheba, he settled there temporarily before he continued his journey to its final destination, which was Egypt. Let's see what Jacob did during his stay in this place. The Bible says,

> And offered sacrifices unto the God of his father Isaac. (Genesis 46:1b)

The attitude of Jacob in the place where he was temporarily established can lead us to ask these questions: Why did Jacob choose to make *sacrifices* to the God of his fathers before his trip to Egypt? What is so special about his actions?

Indeed, Jacob's father was Isaac, who was the son of Abraham (Genesis 21:3). During his lifetime, Abraham walked before the face of the Lord. He was a servant of God (Genesis 12:1-3). Isaac, son of Abraham, also served the Lord (Genesis 26:1-3). That said, there is no doubt that the Lord is the God to whom Jacob offered sacrifices before his trip to Egypt. His father Isaac had served the same God, and his grandfather Abraham also. The action taken by Jacob leads us to understand how some people offer sacrifices to strange gods when they are preparing to leave their country.

On this subject, let me tell you a second anecdote. A young African, for which I prayed a few years ago, told me what happened to him not many days before leaving for the United States. On the eve of his trip, late at night, his mother sat him in front of a large bowl of water full of leaves and roots of trees.

She made him take a bath. During the bath, she explained to her son that she was washing him to be sure to see him again, even if he was leaving the country. Beloved, the Lord invites you to remember your life before your trip. Jacob offered sacrifices to the God of his father before leaving for Egypt. And you, what have you done?

2.3. GOD SPEAKS TO JACOB IN A VISION

> And God spake unto Israel in the visions of the night, and said, Jacob, Jacob. And he said, Here am I. And he said, I am God, the God of thy father: fear not to go down into Egypt; for I will there make of thee a great nation. (Genesis 46:2-3)

To go toward a deity, one must bring an *offering* or sacrifice a victim. For this purpose, Jacob offered sacrifices to the God of his family so that he appeared to him. Through these offerings, Jacob invited the God of his grandfather to reveal himself. After these *holocausts*, the God of Abraham and Isaac appeared to Jacob in a night vision. That being said, when and individual offers sacrifices to a strange god before traveling, he invites a spirit in his life before leaving. Through this spirit, he receives instructions or information necessary for his travel.

In addition, the God who served the ancestors of Jacob and who operated on the spiritual realm was aware of the journey that Jacob was embarking on. He appeared to Jacob in a vision to encourage him to make the trip because the latter was afraid. Despite the word of the king of Egypt and of his sons, Jacob absolutely wanted to consult the God of his family before continuing his journey. Following this consultation, Jacob had the confirmation from God for this move. Some say that the spirits have superior knowledge compared to man. That is why they use spirits as guides. They will burn incense to these strange gods. In return, these spirits confirm their move, direct their trip, teach them how the journey will go, and offer them objects for protection.

Unfortunately, these men and women do not know that from the moment they consulted these gods, they have involved these spiritual forces in the new direction their lives takes. Likewise that the Lord, to whom Jacob offered sacrifices, spoke to him in a vision, these gods who received sacrifices from the hands of these people will appear in dreams to communicate with them.

Let us read again an excerpt from the previous verse in Genesis:

> For I will there make of thee a great nation. (Genesis 46:3b)

As indicated in this verse, that night, Jacob received a promise from the God of his father. The God of his family vowed to bless him in Egypt. Beloved, in the spiritual world, distance is not an obstacle for spiritual forces. These forces can intervene, whether for good or bad, in the life of an individual regardless of the country where he is located. Leaving your nation for another does not mean that you have fled from your family gods or from the gods that you have consulted before your departure. The God of Jacob's family had promised him in a vision that he would multiply him in Egypt. The gods of your family, meaning those to whom you have offered sacrifices before you travel, can promise to achieve the opposite in your life—that is, to bring you to nothing in the country where you want to go. As a result, the situation that you are going through today can be caused by these forces.

2.4.   PROMISES OF GOD TO JACOB

After offering sacrifices to the God of his father, Isaac, Jacob was visited by the Lord in a vision at night. At this moment, God made him four promises concerning future events. Now, let us analyze each of these promises.

In the first promise, God told Jacob that he will make him a nation in Egypt (Genesis 46:3c). People consult their gods when they want to move in order to settle in another land so that these gods bless them in their new nation.

In the second promise, God promised Jacob that he would descend with him into Egypt (Genesis 46:4a). As of then, Jacob, who lived in the physical world, had on the spiritual realm a higher power, the God of his father. The Almighty promised to help, assist, and protect him in Egypt. Beloved, by God's declaration to Jacob, we understand that people who walk in the physical world can be escorted by spirits who are in the spiritual world. Some people are aware of the presence of these spirits that accompany them wherever they go, as Jacob was aware of God's presence around him. There are even those who communicate with these spirits. When people offer sacrifices to strange gods before traveling, they invite these gods by their sacrifices to travel with them. Thus, on the spiritual realm, these gods will follow them on their journey and during their stay. You will understand that the demons immigrate as well as men. Immigration will bring in a country the presence of angels or that of demons.

In the third promise, the Lord asserted to Jacob that he will repatriate him to Egypt (Genesis 46:4b). At this point, Jacob learns that his body will return in Canaan in a coffin. Thousands of men and women would be alive today if they had not left their country for a foreign land, if they had not given sacrifices to strange gods before departure. The land of the nation where they exiled has swallowed them up without them having the opportunity to revisit their home country or their families, as in the case of Naomi's husband and sons that we see in the next section (Ruth 1:1-5). These men and women died and were buried in the nation where they expatriated. Others, having prospered in the territory where they took refuge, returned to their home country in a coffin for burial. It is in a coffin that Joseph brought back Jacob to Canaan. Moreover, it is possible for some to find death when they return to visit their country of birth, after several years of exile.

The God of the fathers of Jacob went to Egypt with Jacob. The Lord told him during his night vision that he himself would be responsible to bring him up again. In the same manner that God confirmed to Israel that he will bring his body in his country, the spirits consulted by some before they travel do the same with the intention to bring back their bodies to their countries of origin. These spirits are therefore responsible for the death of these travelers in a foreign land. If God had assured Jacob that his body would return to his native land, it is because he had already stopped the number of days that Jacob would live in that place.

In the fourth promise, God informs Jacob that his son will close his eyes (Genesis 46:4c). Jacob buried none of his sons; they laid him to the ground. By making connections with the life of Abraham, Isaac, and Jacob, you will see that among these three patriarchs, none has buried their children. However, the reverse is common. Parents see their children die. How many children your father and grandfather have buried? And you, how many children have you already put into the ground?

The following table contains a summary of the four promises in connection with events of everyday life.

Table 3: Summary of the four promises of God to Jacob and spiritual lessons

Promises	Biblical references	Spiritual lessons
1	"For I will there make of thee a great nation" (Genesis 46:3c).	A spirit of the spiritual world can increase someone in his new nation.
2	"I will go down with thee into Egypt" (Genesis 46:4a).	After receiving a sacrifice, a spirit can immigrate with a person in a new country.
3	"And I will also surely bring thee up again" (Genesis 46:4b).	A spirit may be responsible for the return of a person from abroad.
4	"And Joseph shall put his hand upon thine eyes" (Genesis 46:4c).	Spirits can decide where a man will be buried, who will take care of the burial, or who will succeed the deceased.

Before leaving for Egypt, Jacob knew everything that would happen to him during his stay. In the same manner, many will consult spirits to learn about events before they occur. They are seeking to know the future. Like Jacob, you will find people who know what will happen years in advance. However, the question is to know from which sources do they take such information.

2.5.   IS IMMIGRATION A MEANS OF SUCCESS?

In this final section on traveling and ancestral forces, it will be a matter of studying the examples of Jacob and Naomi to discern whether or not immigration is a way to success.

2.5.1.   Jacob's case

In the previous section, we saw that the Lord promised Jacob to make of him a great nation (Genesis 46:3b). Jacob's blessing was not in the land of Canaan; because of that, it was not possible for him to become a great nation in that land. Egypt was the land where the Lord was planning to make him a nation. In this regard, Jacob had immigrated there for this promise to come to pass. The success of Jacob and his family was depending, on one hand, from the forces of the spiritual world, or of the Lord, and on the other hand, of his relocation from Canaan to Egypt.

Whether Christian or not, the wealth enjoyed by humans in this physical world come from the forces that operate in the spiritual world. Likewise, poverty in the life of an individual may occur because some forces in the spiritual realm are opposed to his well-being on earth.

If Jacob had refused to immigrate to Egypt, he would have never tasted the joy set before him as well as for his children. In the case of Jacob, immigration has been a guarantee of success. This is also the same for a number of people. They could not become rich in their country of origin simply because it is not their place of blessing. To succeed, they must leave their homeland for the country that God has chosen for them. Moreover, it is possible that an individual who fails to make ends meet in their country of origin can easily thrive in a foreign land.

2.5.2. Naomi's case (Ruth 1:1-21)

The story of Naomi is found in the book of Ruth. Naomi, her husband, and her children immigrated to the land of Moab due to the famine that was devouring the nation of Judah. Upon arrival in this new territory, her husband died, followed by her two sons. Indeed, as Naomi was in Moab, she heard that the Lord had visited her people and that he had given them bread. That's when she decided to return to her country of origin (Ruth 1:6).

> I went out full and the Lord hath brought me home again empty: why then call ye me Naomi, seeing the Lord hath testified against me, and the Almighty hath afflicted me? (Ruth 1:21)

According to what Naomi declares in Ruth 1:6 and 1:21, we can note two reasons that caused her to leave the country of Moab. First of all, she went back to Bethlehem because her people were visited by God, who gave them bread to eat. Secondly, it was God himself who sent her back to her hometown. Through what Naomi said, we can now understand what happen in the lives of several people who went abroad. Some will decide to return to their home country as soon as there is a political or economical change, while others will go back because they were forced by the powers of darkness to do so.

Naomi said, "The Lord hath brought me home again" (Ruth 1:21b). It seems like it was not the first time she was experiencing this affliction. This enables us to understand that people who use occult powers can send a demon to go and bring back to his home country a person who traveled abroad. In this case, the spirit sent against that fellow will plant in him the desire to go home. That individual will stand up, pack up whatever he's got, and go back to his country. Furthermore, a demon can raise the immigration officers against this person, and they could be deported.

This reminds me of the story of a brother who was living in Germany. This man was married and had a beautiful daughter. One day, he took his passport and left his house for the airport. There, he purchased a ticket and went back to Africa. When he got to his home country, he phoned his wife, who was looking for him, to let her know where he was. This brother suffered for three good years trying to go back to Germany without success until he decided to take counsel from a man of God. According to this minister, a charm was used to call him back home. Beloved, close your eyes and pray like this:

"Any magic power used to call me back home, be struck down by the thunder of God, in the name of Jesus."

That is how Naomi was in abundance before her departure for the land of Moab. Despite the fact that famine struck her land of birth, she enjoyed fairly good living conditions. In Ruth 1:19, we read that the people of the city were moved upon her arrival in Bethlehem because she returned empty-handed and in such bad conditions.

After what happened to Naomi, we can conclude that Moab was not a place of prosperity for Naomi. The favor of God upon her life had not been set out in that nation. Instead, Bethlehem-judah was the place where the blessings of Naomi were. In addition, we saw that the hand of the Lord grew heavier against her in the country where she immigrated. Finally, the God of her family sent her back in her home country empty-handed.

Likewise, some immigrants are reduced to nothing by the gods of their family on their foreign land. They gathered all they had to go abroad, believing to multiply it. Like Naomi, they flourished in their place of birth. However, the hands of the gods to whom they made sacrifices before their departure troubled them in their host country. In poor conditions, these immigrants returned empty-handed to their home country.

In the case of Naomi, immigration had been a big failure because she ignored the principle of blessings management, which is to return to God what he has given us so that he can multiply it, rather than to keep it to ourselves (Genesis 22:12). Naomi took the divine grace received in a fertile soil to go to rejoice in a cursed land. This initiative caused a huge disaster in her life. At first, the misfortune that befell Naomi was similar to what some immigrants experiences today. The prosperity of some individuals is found in their nation. To be blessed, they do not need to leave their home country under the pretext of political or economic crisis.

In the summary table below, we compare the life of Naomi in Bethlehem and in Moab.

Table 4:   Comparison of Naomi's experience in Bethlehem and in Moab

Bethlehem	Moab
Land of birth	Land of immigration
Place of blessings	Place of curses
Place of marriage	Place where she becomes a widow
Place of childbearing	Place of burial of her children
Departure, hands full	Departure, empty-handed

Beloved, if your new homeland is, for you, a place of suffering or has become a furnace the following prayers will rearrange your situation.

2.6. PRAYER SECTION

1. Right hand of the Lord, torment the gods to whom I offered sacrifices before my trip, in the name of Jesus.
2. Divine fire, consume the sacrifices offered to foreign gods the day before my trip, in the name of Jesus.
3. I silence the powers of the mouths that said that I would be cursed in the country where I immigrated, in the name of Jesus.
4. Any god to which my parents have made libation, that wished

   - to feed me with the bread of adversity,
   - to make me drink the water of distress,
   - to make me a useless person in the country where I immigrated,

   fall down flat, in the name of Jesus.

5. Lord, in this country where I immigrated, make me a nation and increase the number of my days, in the name of Jesus.
6. I paralyze the power behind the attacks and the demonic incidents that occurred a few days before my trip, in the name of Jesus.
7. I separate myself from the occult objects that I received before my trip as well as the spirits associated with them, in the name of Jesus.
8. Every spirit that came to talk to me on the eve of my journey through dreams and visions, dry up as the grass on the roof, in the name of Jesus.

9. Any evil objects, used against me in this country, receive double destruction, in the name of Jesus.

10. Lord, destroy the evil objects transported by my enemies from their homeland to the country where they immigrated, in the name of Jesus.

11. I command the ancestral forces that have come with me in the country where I immigrated to go back where they came from, in the name of Jesus.

12. Evil power that came down with me in the country where I immigrated and placed obstacles in my way, be buried by the gravedigger, in the name of Jesus.

13. Every spirit to which I have offered sacrifices before my trip and that

    - visits me in dreams,
    - appears to me in visions,
    - calls me day and night,
    - speaks to me while I am asleep,

    fall and do not rise up, in the name of Jesus.

14. In the name of Jesus, by the power of life, manifested in my tongue, I declare that I will not return in my home country

    - in a coffin,
    - in a wheelchair,
    - empty-handed,
    - with a disease.

15. Any power that came with me in the nation where I immigrated to close my eyes, go into the fire intended for Satan and his angels, in the name of Jesus.

16. I break the curse of death that were made against me and that prevent me from traveling, in the name of Jesus.

17. Let the path of spiritual forces that speak against my trip be dark and slippery, in the name of Jesus.

18. Revoke, Lord, the laws of the spiritual world saying that the day I leave this country, I will die, in the name of Jesus.

19. I shall not return empty-handed, in the name of Jesus.

20. Every power in the spiritual realm, who received orders to snatch my life upon my return from abroad, be pursued by the angel of the Lord, in the name of Jesus.

21. Divine sword, pierce the evil powers of the spiritual realm accompanying me wherever I go, in the name of Jesus.

22. Cursed be the wrath of those who seek after my life because I have traveled, in the name of Jesus.

23. I return the goods and ill-gotten money prior to my trip to the country in which I reside, in the name of Jesus.

24. All prophecy with the mission to cause death, destruction, or failure will come to naught, in the name of Jesus.

25. Bless, O Lord, my departure and my arrival in the country where I am going to live, in the name of Jesus.

26. I break the curses of departure and arrival, in the name of Jesus.

27. My days on the land where I have immigrated will be of 120 years, in the name of Jesus.

28. Any demon with a mission to bring me to my hometown, receive blindness, in the name of Jesus.

29. Any man or woman using a charm to call me back home, you will not succeed, in the name of Jesus.

30. I will not travel under the influence of magic power, in the name of Jesus.

31. I bring the anger of God upon any charm buried under the tree used to call me home, in the name of Jesus.

CHAPTER III

FLYING IN THE DREAMS

I n this chapter, we will discuss flying in the *dreams*. Before we begin, we will deepen our understanding of the phenomenon of dreams.

3.1. THE DREAM

The word *dream* is defined as

> a series of thoughts, images, or emotions occurring during sleep and especially during rapid eye movement (REM) sleep. (*Merriam-Webster Online*, 2013)

The dream or the reverie goes on in the mind of man and concerns the life of the spirit of man during his sleep.

> For God speaketh once, yea twice, yet man perceiveth it not. In a dream, in a vision of the night, when deep sleep falleth upon men, in slumberings upon the bed; Then he openeth the ears of men, and sealeth their

instruction, That he may withdraw man from his purpose, and hide pride from man. (Job 33:14-17)

Through these biblical verses, we learn a dream is one means God uses to speak, warn, and educate people.

As of then, we see the involvement of spiritual forces in dreams. The dream is a way by which spirits, either angels or demons, communicate with humans. While man sleeps on his bed, his physical body is at rest. However, his mind is engaged in actions produced by spiritual forces (angels or demons). Dreams concern human nature and involve the spiritual world. Since God is the creator of all things visible and invisible, let us read his Word in order to understand the reason why people fly in their dreams.

3.2. WHY DO PEOPLE FLY IN THEIR DREAMS?

Flying in dreams appears frequently in man while he is sleeping on his bed. People are regularly seeing themselves flying in the air in their night vision. Some are aware of this; others are not. Is it just a simple experiment? Is there a message behind this activity? Beloved, any experience that takes place in the dreams and that is not of God is an act of the evil one to harm you. Now, let us head in the holy scriptures in the New International Version (NIV) of the Bible, with the book of Job 30:22:

> You snatch me up and drive me before the wind; you
> toss me about in the storm.

Here, the situation that Job was going through was unpleasant. This man lost everything he owned, and as a misfortune does not come alone, his wife decided to leave him in this time of trouble. Then his family and friends moved away from him. Job became an object of mockery for his opponents, a laughingstock. This man, who yesterday was rich, became all of a sudden poor and homeless. He had to sleep in the street, exposed to the weather. His body was full of sores, and his skin stuck to his bones. This man wanted to die. Despite his condition, Job remained clinging to his God he served with strong determination.

Beloved, maybe you are going through a situation similar to that of Job, and you are ready to give up everything because you have lost all hope. Let me bring you good news. This affliction is not in your life to destroy you. In truth, it is for your elevation. Remember what the Epistle of Paul declares to the Ephesians,

And having done all, to stand. (Ephesians 6:13c)

Beloved, you must stand firm.

It was during this unpleasant situation that Job went through a great experience with God. Here is the reason why, when he speaks in this verse, he said, "Thou liftest me up" (Job 30:22a). Here, Job refers to a force present around him and not a man. It was not by his will he was raised but more because of this divine force. Job describes a personal experience. We do not know if this experience took place in the physical world—that is to say, while he was awake or during his sleep, thus in the dream. Nevertheless, here's what we can deduce. We know that Job knew that he had been lifted and that he had no control over this action.

Lift means "to raise from a lower to a higher position: elevate" (*Merriam-Webster Online*, 2013).

Due to this definition, we can conclude that *lift* means taking from the bottom to bring up. Only a force applied to an object can lift it as an elevator or an airplane. For a machine to move from bottom to top, its engine must be turned on. It was the same for Job; a power outside or inside of him took him from the earth to lift him and then to cause him to soar above the wind.

Let us focus our attention on this part of the verse:

Thou causest me to ride upon. (Job 30:22a)

The verb *ride* means the following:

1) To sit and travel on the back of an animal that one directs; 2) To travel as if on a conveyance: be borne; 3) To move like a floating object. (*Merriam-Webster Online*, 2013)

Following this definition, if the action described by Job happened in the physical realm, the force, which had raised him, moved Job above the wind, or it kept him in the air or in space. We thus understand how men move with their physical bodies in the air or the reason why they are held in space. This activity is accomplished by the action of a power. Once a person is being held in the physical space by the action of an evil force, this is levitation. When this power, after lifting him, would move him over the wind, it is telekinesis or teleportation. The danger that will happen to those who practice levitation or teleportation is that they can be spoiled by the storm while doing their experience.

A pastor left Africa for the United States in order to teach about the area of *deliverance* for two weeks. At the end of the training, the pastor asked the congregation if anyone wanted to testify to their experience in the occult or in witchcraft. A young lady stood up to explain what she had experienced when she was five years old. She said that her grandmother was sitting her in front of a pot at around three o'clock in the morning and gave her human *flesh* to eat. Afterward, her grandmother flew all over the house. The experiment described by this young lady happened in the physical world. Undoubtedly, her grandmother used evil powers to fly.

On the other hand, the experience described by Job could have taken place in the spiritual realm while he was on his bed. In his dream, Job saw his spirit moving in the air or maintained in space. Like a dream can be memorized, Job pondered upon waking, in his memory, the film that had happened in his sleep.

Beloved, when in the dream you see yourself move through the air or be maintained in space, this vision shows that around your spirit is a power that lifts you up. It is important to know the power behind this activity on one hand, and on the other hand, to confront it with the prayers that are found at the end of this chapter. Nothing indicates that this act is an initiation into witchcraft. The action takes place in the dream, and some spirits, from the light or darkness, are responsible for that.

3.3. THE CLOUDS

The rapture mentioned by Apostle Paul in 1 Thessalonians 4:17 is similar to the action that describes Job. Let us read this passage:

> Then we which are alive and remain shall be caught up together with them in the clouds, to meet the Lord in the air: and so shall we ever be with the Lord.

Here is one definition of the verb to *catch up*:

> To travel fast enough to overtake an advance party.
> (*Merriam-Webster Online*, 2013)

On the day of the coming of the Lord, men shall be brought up to meet Christ in the air. This abduction will take place through the clouds. This statement of Apostle Paul brings us light on the experience of Job. Now, we have an idea of the force that raised Job and by which he did flow over the wind.

In 1 Thessalonians 4:17, we understand what the people that are transported by the powers of darkness do. They go to meet higher powers who are found on planets, in the atmosphere, or under the sea, to name a few places. Since the living will be removed from the earth in the clouds to meet the Lord in the air, we conclude that it is through a cloud that Job was flying over the wind. Job attributed this activity to God, given his statement in by Job 30:22b, "Thou causeth me to ride upon it," where he addresses the Lord.

Beloved, when you find yourself in the dream, flying in the air, the flight takes place through a cloud on which you are placed. Some may see the cloud, others don't. Because you are not a bird that can fly in the air, to whom will you attribute this activity? Two sources of power can manifest themselves: that of God and that of Satan. Those who believe that the devil is not able to levitate or ride a person in the air are wrong. Let's take a look in the scriptures, in the Gospel according to Matthew 4:5:

> Then the devil taketh him up into the holy city, and
> setteth him on a pinnacle of the temple. (Matthew 4:5)

Here is the explanation of this verse. While he was tempted in the desert after his forty days of fasting, the Lord Jesus was taken by the devil in the desert toward the holy city. He had been brought from the place where he was to another place, not by his power but rather by that of the ancient serpent.

It is through the clouds that men are flying in the wind or levitating. These people, who boast to disappear from one place to appear in another place, are liars. They want to divert the world's attention on the reality of their actions. They do not cease to be visible. Rather, they are transported by the powers of darkness who act in the form of clouds.

3.4. My feet will not glorify Satan

In his night vision, Daniel declares that he saw someone like the Son of man that came on the clouds of heaven (Daniel 7:13). Beloved, in the physical world, people need vehicles to get around. Similarly, in the spiritual world, the spirits make use of clouds to go from one place to another, as indicated by this verse of the book of Daniel. In another passage, King David had a vision of the same situation. It gives us important information that allows us to focus our prayers on one member of our body in particular: our feet. In Psalm 18:9 (NIV), David testifies that he saw the Lord descend from heaven, and dark clouds were under his feet.

In the next table, we see the biblical characters mentioned in this chapter, who flew on clouds and if their activity must be attributed to God or to the enemy.

Table 5:   Biblical characters who flew on clouds and the power responsible

Biblical characters	Biblical references	Power responsible for this activity
Job	"Thou liftest me up to the wind; thou causest me to ride upon it" (Job 30:22a).	God
God	"He parted the heavens and came down; dark clouds were under his feet" (Psalm 18:9, NIV).	God
One like the Son of man	"And, behold, one like the Son of man came with the clouds of heaven" (Daniel 7:13b).	God
Jesus	"Then the devil taketh him up into the holy city, and setteth him on a pinnacle of the temple" (Matthew 4:5).	Satan
Philip (see the section on traveling in chapter 6)	"And when they were come up out of the water, the Spirit of the Lord caught away Philip, that the eunuch saw him no more" (Acts 8:39a).	God
We which are alive	"Shall be caught up together with them in the clouds" (1 Thessalonians 4:17).	God

To conclude, God lifted Job, and Satan took up Jesus. Beloved, if in your dream you see yourself flying through the air, ask the Lord for discernment to know what energy is at the origin of this flight. If it turns out that the devil would have put his clouds (or demons) under your feet, I invite you to pray with holy violence to end this work of the devil in your life. Your feet should glorify God and not the works of darkness. The Lord has given them to you to bring the Gospel throughout the world, not for you to use them on vain, satanic experiences that will ruin your soul. Similarly, in case you have practiced levitation or telekinesis, these warfare and *deliverance* prayers are the solution that will help you to get rid of this situation.

3.5. PRAYER SECTION

1. By the sound of thunder, I destroy the power of Satan that makes me levitate, in the name of Jesus.
2. By the sound of thunder, I neutralize the power of Satan that causes me to ride upon the wind, in the name of Jesus.
3. By the noise of the storm, I tear the evil clouds under the feet of the children of darkness, in the name of Jesus.
4. By the noise of the storm, I crush forces that raise my spirit to keep it in space, in the name of Jesus.
5. By the noise of the storm, I put to flight the forces that raise my spirit to move it on top of the wind, in the name of Jesus.
6. Sword of the Spirit, tear any cloud placed on my feet by the forces of the night, in the name of Jesus.
7. Wing of the wind on which the forces of darkness are hovering, be broken, in the name of Jesus.
8. My spirit, come down from the wind upon which you fly away, in the name of Jesus.
9. I tear up the clouds on which the demons in the air move, in the name of Jesus.
10. My feet, reject the clouds of witchcraft, in the name of Jesus.
11. By the blood of Jesus, I erase the dreams in which I flew in the air, in the name of Jesus.
12. Any evil eagle bearing my spirit on his wings in my dreams, release me and let me go, in the name of Jesus.

13. Any evil scroll flying through the air with my spirit, enough. Withdraw yourself, in the name of Jesus.
14. Scatter, O Lord, the encounter of evil forces in the air, in the name of Jesus.
15. By the power contained in the blood of Jesus, I cancel all evil experience in the air, in the name of Jesus.
16. Angel of Satan carrying my spirit to an unknown destination, be trampled on, in the name of Jesus.
17. Any night bird bringing on its wings my inner man, fall into an evil net, in the name of Jesus.
18. By the stone from the sling, I destroy the evil spirits coming to me in a dark cloud, in the name of Jesus.
19. My spirit, escape from the whirlwind that makes you climb into space, in the name of Jesus.
20. I destroyed the power enabling wizards to fly or to hover on the wind, in the name of Jesus.
21. Any demon that descended from heaven, from the sun, or from the moon, having at its feet a thick cloud, I break your neck, in the name of Jesus.
22. Every power placed on top of my house, come down and be rolled like a stone, in the name of Jesus.
23. Anyone moving at night on a cloud, renounce your evil deeds, in the name of Jesus.
24. Assembly of sorcerers raised in a cloud, return to your homes, in the name of Jesus.
25. Lord, bring down the evil stars that left the East for the top of the place where I live, in the name of Jesus.

CHAPTER IV

EVIL BATHS

This chapter will focus on evil baths, a technique used by Satan and his agents to retain their captives.

4.1. THE SMITH AND THE WASTER

In the book of Isaiah, the Lord made an important statement about our enemy and his activities:

> Behold, I have created the smith that bloweth the coals in the fire, and that bringeth forth an instrument for his work; and I have created the waster to destroy. (Isaiah 54:16)

Satan is the smith, which the Bible refers. He constantly makes weapons of war and affliction. This former covering cherub is persistently working to rise up against God, and all the more, he was cast out of heaven. He works in opposition to the seed of the woman and all those who have the testimony of Jesus Christ. Weapons forged by this serpent are stored in his reserves and distributed to his agents to be used when an opportunity shows up. These instruments, which are so successful in the world, destroy men, women, and children.

These munitions are introduced into the church by wolves through pernicious doctrines. Beloved, Jesus Christ came to destroy the works of darkness. This is why the second part of the verse above announces to us the good news, "And I have created the waster to destroy." The waster comes to shatter the weapon that the smith had made for himself. So no matter where this weapon is directed or used, the waster has the power to locate and destroy them. Beloved, God will not prevent the devil to produce weapons. Our Lord will also not forbid him either to use them against us. Yet what the Lord promises us is to prevent these weapons from flourishing in our lives.

4.2. Baths in the Old Testament

In Exodus 40:12, the Bible declares,

> And thou shalt bring Aaron and his sons unto the door of the tabernacle of the congregation, and wash them with water.

Here are the points that we can draw from this passage:

- Divine instruction: The Lord gave Moses the instruction to purify Aaron and his sons. Moses had not decided to undertake this work. He performed a divine order that had been given unto him.
- Instruction from the spiritual world: The action of Moses on Aaron and his sons came from the spiritual

world. He was in the physical realm, while the Creator who spoke to him was in the spiritual realm.

- Place of bath: The instruction was given to Moses to wash his brother and his nephews in front of the tabernacle of the congregation. The Almighty had chosen the place where these people should be washed. The fact that this bath was held before the tabernacle of the congregation demonstrates that there was nothing wrong behind this action.

- Time of bath: Moses was to administer the bath in broad daylight, such as we receive confirmation through the declaration of the Lord in John 9:4. Our Father always acts in transparency. This bath had to be seen by the children of Israel to make them aware of the plans of the Lord for his servants.

- Pronunciation: The Lord had not commanded Moses to utter words while he bathes Aaron and his sons.

- Divine presence: The presence of the Lord was around the *tabernacle* and the tabernacle of the congregation; consequently, it was before God that this bath was held.

- Object of purification: Moses was instructed to only purify them with water. The water used for the occasion was not to be mixed with another product.

4.3. How did the prophet intended to conduct this bath?

The question we must ask ourselves is how Moses was considering carrying out this bath. Aaron was eighty-three years old (Exodus 7:7). His sons were certainly men of middle age. Did Moses have to wash Aaron and his sons naked in front of the tabernacle of the congregation? What would have people thought of this gesture? Is it not strange to see an old man cleaning another in his Adam's outfit? Have those who do this type of bath lost their mind or reason?

4.4. THE ACTION OF THE LORD ON HIS DISCIPLES

To understand how Moses proceeded to purify Aaron and his children, let us examine what the Lord did to His disciples:

> After that he poureth water into a basin, and began to wash the disciples' feet, and to wipe them with the towel wherewith he was girded. Jesus saith to him, He that is washed needeth not save to wash his feet, but is clean every whit: and ye are clean, but not all. (John 13:5-10)

This said, that washing the Lord did to his disciples is the image of the command Moses received from God in the Old Testament. In the two preceding verses, the Bible only mentions the washing of feet. In this story, even when Peter insisted that his hands and head be washed, the Lord Jesus refused him (John 13:9).

With this information, we can assume that Moses did not expose his older brother's nakedness nor that of his nephews' to bathe them; he washed their feet instead.

4.5. THE PURPOSE OF BATHS IN THE OLD AND THE NEW TESTAMENTS

Generally, in the Old and New Testaments, baths are made for the same reasons. The scriptures show a resemblance between what God did with the prophets and what Jesus achieved when he was on earth. In the Old Testament, the baths were used for the purification and the sanctification of those who had to work for the Lord (Exodus 40:12-15). It was the same when the Lord Jesus washed his disciples' feet. The issue was to cleanse them because they had been chosen to bring the Gospel to the world (Matthew 28:16-20 and John 13:10). A second use of baths in the Old and the New Testaments is found in the context of healing (2 Kings 5:10 and John 9:6-7).

4.6.   REPROVE THE WORKS OF DARKNESS

> And have no fellowship with the unfruitful works of darkness, but rather reprove them. (Ephesians 5:11)

The Bible recommends us to walk in a manner worthy of the Lord and to be pleasing unto him, bearing fruits in every good work. Furthermore, it commands us to reprove these evil deeds. Here, two actions must be taken by a Christian: first, he must reject anything that comes from the devil then he must rigorously disapprove the works of darkness. Indeed, we disobey the Word of God by rejecting the works of darkness, without blaming them. Likewise, stigmatizing the works of the enemy and then taking part in them is not what God expects of us.

Beloved, it is possible that a false prophet in sheep's clothing advises that you pour oil in water, which he will call anointing oil, and read Bible verses while taking your bath. Ask him to show you this practice in the Word of God. Since he will not be able to prove it, you will thereafter condemn this work. Although a false prophetess would tell you to go wash at midnight at a crossroad to change your situation, do not participate in this work. You will notice the following representations:

- Demonic inspiration: It is under the inspiration or under the order of a demon that this false prophet has spoken to you. An unclean spirit would have used this latter to ask you to go take this bath.
- Place of bath: The place where you will take the bath is chosen by the evil spirit that speaks through the false prophet. God commanded Moses to wash Aaron in front of the tent of the congregation. Similarly, these evil spirits, through these prophets send their customers to take baths at various locations, such as at the edge of rivers, in cemeteries, at crossroads, behind a house during the full moon, to name a few.
- Demonic presence: A demon is already in these places when you wash. It is before this demon that you display your nakedness.
- Person who administers the bath: The cleverest of these false prophets will offer themselves to wash their client, such as Moses did for Aaron and his sons.
- Consecration: While these liars wash their customer by uttering imprecations, they devote that person to their demon or to their foreign god. This person is unaware that he or she is purified to become the property of another deity.
- Repercussions: Finally, during this type of bath, the false prophet and his client, out of clumsiness, could fall into *adultery* or fornication.

The next table compares various activities depending on whether the bath is inspired by God or the devil.

Table 6: Divine bath versus demonic bath

Activities	Divine bath	Demonic bath
Source of the instruction	Inspired by God	Inspired by Satan
Person who administers the bath	A man of God	A false prophet
Place of bath	Before the tabernacle of the congregation	By riverbanks, in cemeteries, at crossroads, behind a house during the full moon, in temples, or in homes
Time of bath	In broad daylight	Often at night (may also occur during the day or early in the morning)
Pronunciation	None	Utter obscure words or Bible verses
Presence	Divine	Demonic
Object of purification	Water	Counterfeit "anointing oil" with the bones from an animal, a coin in water, or another object given by the sorcerer
Consecration	To God	To a demon or to a strange god
Repercussions	Be pure for God's service	Can often cause people to fall into sin or to be possessed by a spirit

4.7. VARIOUS TYPES OF EVIL BATHS

In this section, we will discuss the baths performed with evil soaps, salt baths, blood baths, and Muslim baths.

4.7.1. Baths with evil soaps (Job 9:30-31)

> Even if I washed myself with soap and my hands
> with cleansing powder, you would plunge me into a
> slime pit so that even my clothes would detest me.
> (Job 9:30-31, NIV)

In this passage, the soap spoken by Job did not have the potential
to make him pure before the face of God. Its use would have
led to contamination in the life of Job, and the Lord would have
shied away from him. Beloved, to be purified, we need the Word
of God and prayer as the scriptures would confirm it to us,

> For it is sanctified by the word of God and prayer. (1
> Timothy 4:5)

No prophet in the Bible has given soap to someone to use under
the pretext that God will answer their queries. At first glance,
according to Job 9:30-31, a person using a soap that was given
to him from the hands of a false prophet will attract the wrath of
the Lord against him. The user of this evil soap will be plunged
into a slime pit. His clothes will be affected by the pollution and
would detest him or become his enemy. This is one of the reason
why it's not a good idea to wear somebody else's clothes. Such
act can bring pollution or affliction in one's life. In addition, he
will be horrible, unclean, until the day when he will seek the face
of God Almighty. Beloved, if you use one of these soaps, you'd
better get rid of it immediately. Ask the Lord to cleanse you from
the defilements introduced into your body because of this soaps.

An African woman who was tired of suffering decided to take
charge of her destiny. She went to seek help from a witch
doctor in hope that her life would change. She received from

the latter a paste soap in a pot like a calabash for the bath. Being a manager in a bar, this woman noticed a rapid change manifested in her life. The use of this soap led people to be favorable toward her, and her financial situation was restored. Yet several years later, this lady realized she was confronted with another problem. Now she had squandered her money without her being able to achieve concrete projects with her equity.

4.7.2.   Salt baths (Jeremiah 2:22)

> For though thou wash thee with nitre, and take thee much soap, yet thine iniquity is marked before me, saith the Lord God. (Jeremiah 2:22)

To fully grasp this verse, let's look at some definitions.

The word *nitre* specifies "niter" (*Merriam-Webster Online*, 2013).

The word *niter* means "potassium nitrate" (*Merriam-Webster Online*, 2013).

The term *potassium nitrate* signifies, "a crystalline salt KNO_3 that is a strong oxidizing agent and is used in medicine chiefly as a diuretic—called also niter, saltpeter" (*Merriam-Webster Online*, 2013).

At the end, nitre is salt.

A quick glance at the Bible verse above in Jeremiah 2:22 allows us to clearly understand that the Lord Almighty refers to people who use evil salt baths for the purification of their body or to solve their problems. Beloved, it is a sin before God for an individual to pour water into a basin or bucket and then introduce salt in it to take a bath. God informs us that this sin will remain marked in front of him. Verily if you are engaged in such activity, you must promptly return to your God to ask him for forgiveness so that he delivers you from the hands of the enemy that is holding you captive. Do not be fooled by these false prophets who will tell you that we are the salt of the earth and as a result you can bathe with salt. This doctrine is of the devil and not of scriptures. If God wanted to make your physical body salty, he would have made you a codfish, the salted fish of the sea!

Beloved, bathing with salt will not take your iniquity away, bring any change in your life, or deliver you from evil; only the Word of God it able to do so (Psalm 107:20). A sister who was going through some difficulties decided to open her heart to a believer, who she thought was a mature Christian. After explaining what her trouble was, the so-called Christian advised her to go home and take a salt bath. He told her that while taking this bath, she must cry unto God to deliver her from evil.

4.7.3. Blood baths (1 Kings 22:38)

King Ahab went to war against the Syrians with King Jehoshaphat. The battle increased, to the point where King Ahab died from an injury that shed his blood in the chariot. Thereafter the servants of this dead king came, took his body out of the chariot, and went to wash the tank in the pool of Samaria. The blood of the king spread throughout the pond.

> And one washed the chariot in the pool of Samaria;
> and the dogs licked up his blood; and they washed
> his armour; according unto the word of the Lord
> which he spake. (1 Kings 22:38)

The same verse in the New King James Version (NKJV) of the Bible says,

> Then someone washed the chariot at a pool in Samaria, and the dogs licked up his blood while the harlots bathed, according to the word of the Lord which He had spoken. (1 Kings 22:38, NKJV)

Prostitutes came to bathe in this water mixed with human blood. These have had a blood bath. Their physical bodies were soaked with human blood. So they all entered the same blood covenant. At the present time, just like these prostitutes, people take blood baths following the recommendation of false prophets who wish to satisfy their master, Satan.

Another type of blood bath is described in the book of Leviticus 8:30. In this verse, God recommends Moses to take the anointing oil and the blood, which was upon the altar, and to sprinkle it on Aaron, his sons, and their clothes so that they can be sanctified. The blood that Moses took on the altar was the one of the rams. From this example, we discover another type of evil bath practiced by the children of disobedience. During some rituals, animals like goats, oxen, or chickens are slaughtered in order to collect their blood to pour on humans or wash them. Once this bath takes place in the life of a person, this one will be automatically chained by the devil.

4.7.4. Baths of the Muslim religion

> Peter saith unto him, Thou shalt never wash my feet. Jesus answered him, If I wash thee not, thou hast no part with me. Simon Peter saith unto him, Lord, not my feet only, but also my hands and my head. Jesus

saith to him, He that is washed needeth not save to wash his feet, but is clean every whit: and ye are clean, but not all. (John 13:8-10)

By analyzing these verses, we can draw the following conclusions. First, the idea of purification by washing hands, head, and feet came from Peter. The Lord rebuked Peter by rejecting this manner of sanitation. Thereafter the Lord showed Peter the method to follow to become pure. Finally, the purification allows an individual to be rewarded by a deity.

In addition, supporters of the Muslim religion follow the method of Peter that consists of washing the head, hands, and feet whenever they wish to purify themselves. Yet the Lord has rejected this way. In Mark 8:33, the Lord rebuked Peter sharply by ordering him, "Get thee behind me, Satan."

It is likely that Satan still wanted to use Peter to divert God's plan. Similarly, whenever a Muslim washes his hands, head, and feet, he does so to have to share in a reward from a god who is not the one who created the heavens and the earth. This follower engages in an evil bath. By this gesture, he worships the spirit that spoke through the mouth of Peter. A Christian, who was a Muslim in the past, must break the yoke of this evil spirit in his life.

4.7.5.   Baths in streams

Naaman was a man of war, a military leader afflicted with leprosy. He left his country, Syria, for Samaria in order to meet Elisha the prophet. Naaman wanted to cure from this disease. Prophet Elisha gave this military leader an instruction inspired by the Holy Spirit:

> So Naaman came with his horses and with his
> chariot, and stood at the door of the house of Elisha.
> And Elisha sent a messenger unto him, saying, Go
> and wash in Jordan seven times, and thy flesh shall
> come again to thee, and thou shalt be clean. (2 Kings
> 5:9-10)

God decided to heal this man in the waters of Jordan. In verse
14 of the same chapter, the Bible says that Naaman dipped
himself seven times in Jordan River, according to the word of
Elisha, and he became pure. Naaman acted by faith, and he
received his *deliverance*, for an angel of God had passed to stir
the water of the Jordan a few minutes before (John 5:4).

At the moment, fake pastors infiltrated in the church practice
healing through bathing in the river. They recommend their
followers to wash in the river on the pretext that they will be
healed or delivered from the hands of the forces behind their
problem. In fact, by what spirit are they talking? When their
followers perform what they were advised, they open a breach
for Satan in their lives through this evil bath. Now the water
spirits will be invited to invade the lives of these people. Elisha
did not wash Naaman in River Jordan. Jesus did not go to the
pool of Siloam to wash the blind man for him to regain his
sight.

Beloved, some of you, one way or another, have taken evil baths
either through ignorance or under constraint. It is not too late.
God has the power to deliver you, only if you desire it.

Now, I invite you to do the following prayers with holy anger
so that the forces that entered into your life through these
demonic baths must be confused and flee through different

ways. Our God is a battle axe and a weapon of war. He is ready to intervene in our lives whenever we cry out to him for help.

4.8. PRAYER SECTION

1. Let all blood baths affecting my body be destroyed, in the name of Jesus.
2. Blood of goats and chickens sprinkled on my body in a ritual, lose your power, in the name of Jesus.
3. I break the covenants in which I entered through blood baths, in the name of Jesus.
4. Voice of the blood of animals used in evil baths shouting against me, silence. Be still, in the name of Jesus.
5. Any man who desires my blood or that of my children to take an evil bath be judged by your conscience, in the name of Jesus.
6. Fire of the Holy Ghost, consume the basins and the sponges used by my enemies in evil baths, in the name of Jesus.
7. Destroy, O Lord, the soaps used in evil baths, in the name of Jesus.
8. I destroy the power of those who take baths with evil soap to veil my intelligence or to seduce me, in the name of Jesus.
9. I destroy the power of those who take baths with evil soap to bewitch me or to dominate me, in the name of Jesus.
10. I destroy the power of those who take baths with evil soap to confront or to resist me, in the name of Jesus.
11. By the blood of Jesus, I destroy the pollution of the soaps used to purify my body, to bring me favor, or to protect me, in the name of Jesus.

12. Any unclean spirit plunging me in the mire because of the evil soaps I have used, be rolled like a ball, in the name of Jesus.

13. I destroy and I get rid of the soaps given to me by false prophets, in the name of Jesus.

14. Every demon in the spiritual world declaring that my blood will serve to bathe prostitutes, swallow your words, in the name of Jesus.

15. Any false prophet cleansing his hands with evil soap in order to work miracles, I disgrace your evil anointing, in the name of Jesus.

16. Destroy, O Lord, the affliction in my life caused by the use of evil soaps, in the name of Jesus.

17. By the blood of Jesus, I exterminate the evil perfumes of soaps used to purify my body, in the name of Jesus.

18. By the blood of Jesus, I exterminate the odors of the evil soaps that cause rejection in my life, in the name of Jesus.

19. Every demon present during evil baths that occurred at intersections, in rivers, in cemeteries, behind the houses, in temples, or in the forest, flee seven ways, in the name of Jesus.

20. Every demon present during blood baths, salt baths and evil soap baths, be put into chains by the angel of the Lord, in the name of Jesus.

21. Every elemental forces that controls my life since I've made an evil bath, be pulled out, in the name of Jesus.

22. I bind and I chase the marine spirits that came into my life after I dipped myself seven times in the rivers, in the name of Jesus.

23. I bind and I chase the evil spirits that possess my physical body through evil baths, in the name of Jesus.

24. Lord, place a heavy yoke on the neck of the genies of the soothsayers taking evil baths before the preparation of rituals or fetishes against my person, in the name of Jesus.

25. I cancel the recommendation of the false prophets that advised me to immerse myself seven times in the river, in the name of Jesus.

26. Any demon, which uses the false prophet's mouth to entice me to take an evil bath, eat the dust, in the name of Jesus.

27. Lord, shake the power of the hands that went through my body during evil baths, in the name of Jesus.

28. I cancel every consecration to strange gods through evil baths, in the name of Jesus.

29. Any foreign god to whom I have been offered during evil baths, be pierced by arrows, in the name of Jesus.

30. I bind the obscure words that I have pronounced during evil baths, in the name of Jesus.

31. I bind the magic words uttered by wicked people during evil baths, in the name of Jesus.

32. By the blood of Jesus, I erase the sins caused by salt baths, in the name of Jesus.

33. Forgive me, Lord, for having washed myself with salt. May this iniquity be erased from before thee, in the name of Jesus.

34. By the blood of Jesus, I erase from the memory of forces of darkness, the evil salt baths that I took, in the name of Jesus.

35. I break the covenants made with the world of darkness through evil salt baths, in the name of Jesus.

36. Demonic salt used for the purification of my body, lose your flavor in my life, in the name of Jesus.

37. I shake off my body the salt used in evil baths, in the name of Jesus. *(Link action to speech while you pray.)*

38. Evil salt planted in my life through satanic baths, be damaged, in the name of Jesus.
39. Angel of the Lord, strike the powers that have used salt baths to limit me, in the name of Jesus.
40. Let the power behind the baths of the Muslim religion be confounded and be put to shame in my life, in the name of Jesus.
41. By the power of the Holy Spirit, I destroy any substance, such as salt or oil, mixed into water by my enemies, before they take a bath, in the name of Jesus.

CHAPTER V

CONFRONTING THE EVIL SPIRIT OF YOUR UNCLE

The Bible attests to which manner the sins of a father can affect the lives of his children and grandchildren unto the fourth generation (Exodus 20:5). In addition, the Word of God tells us that a mother can give birth to a child and then eat that baby (2 Kings 6:28-29). These examples are intended to help us understand that our parents may be responsible for the problems that disturb our lives.

In his Word, God did not limit himself to point the finger at our fathers and mothers. Indeed, he went further by adding other members of our families to consider as our enemies—in this case, uncles and aunts.

5.1. THE FACE-OFF

Laban, the Syrian, was the uncle of Jacob. He was the brother of Rebekah, Jacob's mother. The parents of Jacob, Isaac and Rebekah, advised him to go to his uncle Laban to find a wife. Moreover, his departure allowed him to get away from his brother Esau, who wanted to kill him.

> And it came to pass, when Rachel had born Joseph, that Jacob said unto Laban, Send me away, that I may go unto mine own place, and to my country. Give me my wives and my children, for whom I have served thee, and let me go: for thou knowest my service which I have done thee. And Laban said unto him, I pray thee, if I have found favour in thine eyes, tarry: for I have learned by experience that the Lord hath blessed me for thy sake. (Genesis 30:25-27)

Beloved, it is difficult to admit that the people you love the most are often the ones that prevent you from moving forward. Great will be your surprise the day you will have this type of revelation. Where will you go? And what will you do? You will not believe what you see or hear. It is at this moment that the following questions will fill your mind: How is it that my uncle is a stumbling block in my life, did he really act against my progress? What have I done to deserve my aunt's anger?

In connection with what is written above, the Bible says, "The heart is deceitful above all things, and desperately wicked: who can know it?" (Jeremiah 17:9).

If Jacob had known the condition of the heart of his uncle before his trip, he would never have fled in his home. In addition, it is certain that his mother did not know who her brother really was; otherwise, she would not have offered her son to undertake this journey.

However, the birth of Joseph brought in Jacob's life, his father, the deliverance from the bonds in which he was held. This man, who yesterday could not raise his voice before his uncle, was released from the fear that he infused in him. The veil that Laban had put on the face of Jacob was torn.

Let us read again carefully what the following passage recounts:

> And it came to pass, when Rachel had born Joseph, that Jacob said unto Laban, Send me away, that I may go unto mine own place, and to my country. (Genesis 30:25)

Following the birth of his son Joseph, Jacob took back all his senses. In his mind, he went over the film of all the atrocities he endured because of his uncle during all these years. Laban's manipulation was laid bare.

In the same vein, the birth of Joseph for Jacob is similar to that of John the Baptist for his father (Luke 1:57-64). Zacharias, the father of John the Baptist, was mute. The latter saw his tongue loosen eight days after the birth of his son. The bit that held his mouth shut was taken away by the power of God during the ceremony where the baby receives his name on the eighth day after his birth. By examining the case of these two patriarchs, we can say that the power of deliverance of the Lord manifested in the life of his servants at the birth of a child in a family. God has not changed. He is the same yesterday and today and will remain the same tomorrow. What he has done with Jacob and Zacharias, he can also perform it in our lives.

5.2. "Send me away"

Jacob's statement to his uncle, "Send me away," shows that Laban kept him captive. This man kept his nephew prisoner. He had reduced his sister's son to a slave. Laban was sitting on Jacob, thus holding back his freedom. Laban became the strongman in the life of his son-in-law. Consequently, the son of Rebekah no longer wished to serve his uncle. It was time for him to move forward in his life. He was tired of being exploited by the Syrian, who was using him to his advantage and utilized his efforts to thrive. This man did not respect his nephew. He was solely interested in the gain that he obtained by forcing Jacob to work for him.

Here's what some of our uncles represent in our families. They abuse the children of their brothers as soon as these come to them seeking help or asking for advice. These uncles are using the ignorance of their nephews to control their lives. These Labans use their powers to sit upon the destiny of their Jacobs and retain their nephews chained to prevent them from moving forward.

In our time, many people suffer from their ignorance. They do not know that the strongman in their life is this uncle or aunt that they call regularly to ask for help or advice.

The cry of Jacob, "Send me away," is an expression of warfare. It is used by those who want to get out of the furnace in which they were placed by their executioner, those who are willing to confront the forces that resist their destiny, those who are called to fight against spiritual forces, those who do not give up in a difficult situation, those who do not lay down their arms before the fight is over, and those who know that through God they shall do valiantly.

In the Old Testament, a similar expression was used by God while the people of Israel were held captive by the Egyptians. God sent Moses to Pharaoh to order him to let his people go

(Exodus 8:1). Beloved, for the strongman sitting on your life to let you go, you will have to confront him. The birth of Joseph allowed Jacob to seize this need for confrontation. So he decided to fight for his life and his family.

5.3.   "GIVE ME MY WIVES AND MY CHILDREN"

In this case, Jacob ordered his uncle to give him his wives and children (Genesis 30:26). Laban had taken everything that Jacob had. He had swallowed up the goods of his nephew. Jacob was stripped and emptied by his uncle. Even though Jacob had children, he had no parental rights over his offspring. While he had wives, he could not enjoy them. His uncle had made his life miserable. While Jacob worked, Laban was blessed. Let us read the following verse, which is the declaration of Laban to his nephew:

> These daughters are my daughters, and these children
> are my children, and these cattle are my cattle, and
> all that thou seest is mine. (Genesis 31:43b)

Laban had proclaimed himself the owner of the property of Jacob. According to him, all that belonged to Jacob was his. This is another feature identified in some of our uncles. These uncles are only emptiers and dragons. They have a belly full of goods that do not belong to them. Their houses are full of deceit. They are brilliantly overweight. They exceed all measure of evil.

Beloved, maybe your uncle is holding your marriage, which explains why you are still single. It is probably that man who holds your children or your belly; that is why you do not give birth. This uncle is the one who emptied you of all your physical, moral, and spiritual potentials. Even though it is possible that your work and your finances are held by this uncle, do not be discouraged, for God gives you hope in this scripture:

> Woe to thee that spoilest, and thou wast not spoiled; and dealest treacherously, and they dealt not treacherously with thee! when thou shalt cease to spoil, thou shalt be spoiled; and when thou shalt make an end to deal treacherously, they shall deal treacherously with thee. (Isaiah 33:1)

Here is one of the great promises that God gives us in his Word. These uncles will be treated the way they treated you. After having completed to spoil and deal with their nephews treacherously, in turn, they will be plundered and ravaged. They will not go unpunished for their crimes.

5.4.　WHO WAS REALLY LABAN?

Laban, mystical figure and petty, full of plunder, enemy of progress, was the uncle of Jacob as well as his father-in-law. In addition, this man had other personalities. The different identities of Laban are those of a *traditional chief*, a dualist, and a servant of images.

5.4.1.　Laban was a traditional chief

The word *tradition* is defined as the following:

> 1) An inherited, established, or customary pattern of thought, action, or behavior (as a religious practice or a social custom); 2) A belief or story or a body of beliefs or stories relating to the past that are

commonly accepted as historical though not verifiable. (*Merriam-Webster Online*, 2013)

As for the word *chief* it means

Accorded highest rank or office. (*Merriam-Webster Online*, 2013)

Laban insisted that the rules of the tradition, of which he was the chief, were met.

And Laban said, It must not be so done in our country, to give the younger before the firstborn. (Genesis 29:26)

Laban applied the custom when he gave Leah for marriage to Jacob instead of Rachel, the younger sister of Leah. However, the Word of God denounces these rites: "Making the word of God of none effect through your tradition" (Mark 7:13a).

As a result of reading this verse, we deduce that the custom and the Word of God do not agree at all. Thus, those who are attached to the folklore are entirely drifting away from the Lord. Consequently, Jacob had married in a family governed by tradition.

5.4.2.   Laban was a dualist

In addition, Jacob's uncle was in favor of dualism. His religious ideas admitted two opposing principles. Let us read what Laban and his father stated when Abraham's servant came and asked Rebekah to marry Isaac.

> Then Laban and Bethuel answered and said, The thing proceedeth from the Lord: we cannot speak unto thee bad or good. (Genesis 24:50)

Laban and his father claim that the mission of Abraham's servant came from the Lord, and in return, they could not oppose it. Also, let us read now what Laban said, after his nephew Jacob had fled, in relation to their meeting at mount Gilead.

> And now, though thou wouldest needs be gone, because thou sore longedst after thy father's house, yet wherefore hast thou stolen my gods? And Jacob answered and said to Laban, Because I was afraid: for I said, Peradventure thou wouldest take by force thy daughters from me. (Genesis 31:30-31)

In the presence of Abraham's servant and his family members and during the wedding of his sister, Laban made an allusion to the Lord. On another occasion, when he was in conflict with his nephew, Laban sought his gods. On one hand, this man recognized the power of the Lord; on the other hand, he had not renounced the power of Satan.

5.4.3. Laban served graven images

Let us read the passage below:

> And now, though thou wouldest needs be gone, because thou sore longedst after thy father's house, yet wherefore hast thou stolen my gods? (Genesis 31:30)

Laban accuses Jacob of the disappearance of his gods. However, of which gods was he really talking about?

And Laban went into Jacob's tent, and into Leah's tent, and into the two maidservants' tents; but he found them not. Then went he out of Leah's tent, and entered into Rachel's tent. Now Rachel had taken the images, and put them in the camel's furniture, and sat upon them. And Laban searched all the tent, but found them not. (Genesis 31:33-34)

The gods to which Laban refers were *theraphim*, which is defined as follows:

A) Images. A household god thought to guard and guide the home and its family affairs. B) Usually a statue or a figurine. Judges 17:5 and 18:4, 17-18; Hosea 3:4 (Price 2006, p. 555)

It seems obvious to us that Laban was a servant of Satan. Jacob's uncle worshiped strange gods. Consequently, the spirit of these theraphim or household gods was living inside him because he was attached to it (1 Corinthians 6:17-19). It is this spirit that hardened the heart of Laban against Jacob so that he made his nephew miserable.

Meanwhile, the same scenario occurred with Judas Iscariot. Indeed, when the devil entered into Judas, he went along with the chief priests on how to deliver the Lord Jesus into their hands (Luke 22:2-4).

5.5.   WHAT TO DO DURING THIS CONFRONTATION?

The Bible commands us not to fight against flesh and blood—that is to say, against human beings (Ephesians 6:12). Jacob's struggle was not to be conducted against Laban, his uncle. By confronting him, he struggled against flesh and blood. In most cases, men act similarly to Jacob. From the moment they know that this uncle or that aunt is responsible for such bad situations in their lives or in the family, they will physically confront them. This sort of confrontation occurs by the works of the flesh.

The same verse of Ephesians 6:12 prescribes that our wrestling match must be more focused against principalities, against power, against the rulers of the darkness of this world, and against spiritual wickedness in high places. Whatever anyone says, Jacob had to confront the spirits that dwelt in his uncle and not his uncle himself. These principalities and these authorities of which the Bible refers are spirits that have the ability to enter the body of an individual to use him and to get out of this body once their mission is accomplished.

In the New Testament, Jesus severely rebuked Peter and replied:

> Get thee behind me, Satan: for thou savourest not the things that be of God, but the things that be of men. (Mark 8:33b)

Jesus confronted the enemy who was inside Peter. This spirit that had entered Peter was using his thoughts so that the Lord would turn away from his mission.

Beloved, resist by prayer the evil spirit living in your uncle or your aunt from working against you. Once this spirit is crushed, the hand of that person may not destroy you. God, who threatened Laban concerning Jacob (Genesis 31:24), has not changed. He will do the same concerning you. The Lord will bring judgment between you and your uncle. He will overthrow the gods of the home of this member of your family and take away their yoke from your neck. Finally, I invite you, through this session of prayers, to stand up and confront the evil spirit that inhabits this uncle or this aunt. Otherwise, they will always keep you in captivity. God is giving to you an opportunity to understand those explanations so that you will be free from the hands of the gods that serve your uncle or your aunt. It took twenty years for Jacob to understand. Do not wait so long. Today, God will set you free.

5.6. PRAYER SECTION

1. Angel of the Lord, pursue the evil spirit of my uncle who runs after me, in the name of Jesus.
2. Witchcraft spirit of my uncle and my aunt pursuing me, be broken to pieces, in the name of Jesus.
3. Divine hammer, shatter the graven images and occult objects found in the houses of my uncles and aunts, in the name of Jesus.
4. Any evil object that was moved from my uncle's home to my house, wherever you are, receive your destruction, in the name of Jesus.
5. Lord, destroy the strange gods that my uncles brought into my home, in the name of Jesus.
6. Evil spirit inhabiting my uncle body and opposing to my marriage, my finances, and my progress, be thrown like a stone into the sea, in the name of Jesus.
7. I destroy the evil thoughts in the heart of my aunt who wants to seduce my husband, in the name of Jesus.
8. I destroy the evil thoughts in the heart of my uncle who wants to seduce my wife, in the name of Jesus.
9. Divine chariot of fire, separate my uncle from his strange gods, in the name of Jesus.

10. By the power of the Holy Spirit, I declare, "The mouths of my uncles or my aunts will speak neither good nor bad of me, in the name of Jesus."

11. Lord, in the name of Jesus, overthrow the powers that

   - harden the heart of my uncles against me,
   - prevent my uncles to let me go,
   - trigger my uncles to raise their hands against me,
   - strengthen the arms of my uncles.

12. By the Word of God, I cancel the custom of my ancestors as well as their works in my life, in the name of Jesus.

13. Let there be war in my family between God's angels and the spirits of the custom, in the name of Jesus.

14. I destroy the laws of custom applied in my family by my uncles, in the name of Jesus.

15. I plunder and havoc the evil spirits living in my uncle, in the name of Jesus.

16. Lord, let misfortunes fall upon the strange gods that my uncles and my aunts are serving, in the name of Jesus.

17. Feet of the witchcraft spirit inhabiting the body of my uncle, be removed from my finances, in the name of Jesus.

18. Hand of witchcraft spirit inhabiting the body of my uncle and holding my womb, dry up and be cut off, in the name of Jesus.

19. Spirit of witchcraft inhabiting the body of my aunt, release me and let me go, in the name of Jesus.

20. Lord, prevent the evil powers of my uncles to afflict me, in the name of Jesus.

21. Lord, cause a great earthquake and let the evil objects buried in the yard of my uncles for protection be shattered, in the name of Jesus.

22. Any demon, obstinate to take what belongs to me to give to my uncles, be transformed into salt, in the name of Jesus.

23. Lord, see everything that my uncles are doing to me, in the name of Jesus.

24. My soul, arise and get out from my uncle's house or cage, in the name of Jesus.

25. I get out from my uncle's house with all that belongs to me, in the name of Jesus.

26. Angel of the Lord, appear in the night in a dream to my uncle and command him to let me go and give me what belongs to me, in the name of Jesus.

27. Let the force that's strengthening my uncle's hand be rendered powerless, in the name of Jesus.

28. Let the gods of my uncles, who want me to return empty, perish, in the name of Jesus.

29. Any uncle searching my life and my effects will not find anything, in the name of Jesus.

30. Familiar spirits of my uncle who steal from me during the day, be consumed by the heat, in the name of Jesus.

31. Familiar spirits of my uncle who steal from me during the night, be devoured by the cold, in the name of Jesus.

32. Lord, pronounce your judgment between me and my uncles, in the name of Jesus.

33. Thou wicked uncle confessing that my wife, children, and property are his, I bind the words of thy mouth, in the name of Jesus.

34. I break the evil covenants between me and my uncles, in the name of Jesus.

35. Any evil stone used in a covenant between my uncles and me, be crushed, in the name of Jesus.

36. All food I ate in an evil covenant with my uncles, be expelled from my stomach, in the name of Jesus.

37. Any food that has been used to seal an evil covenant between my aunt and me, be destroyed in my stomach, by the power of God, in the name of Jesus.

38. Any strange gods protecting my uncles, be devoured by wild beasts, in the name of Jesus.

39. By the blood of Jesus, I cancel the blessings pronounced upon me by those who serve strange gods in my family, in the name of Jesus.

40. Names of the gods invoked by my uncles, be erased by the blood of Jesus, in the name of Jesus.

41. Jars of clay in the house of my uncle containing my properties, filled with evil, be broken into pieces, in the name of Jesus.

42. Lord, reduce to nothing the counsel of witchcraft of my uncles, in the name of Jesus.

43. Lord, destroy on my behalf the witchcraft counsel of my aunts, in the name of Jesus.

44. Houses of the gods of my uncles, be demolished, in the name of Jesus.

45. Any stone or evil object hanging in the house of my uncle / my aunt, fall down and be broken, in the name of Jesus.

46. Idol of my uncle's house, fall and rise no more, in the name of Jesus.

47. Lion of the tribe of Judah, pursue the spirits sent against me by my uncles, in the name of Jesus.

CHAPTER VI

ACCIDENTS CAUSED BY THE SPIRITUAL WORLD (PART 1)

The issue of accidents caused by the spiritual world contains two chapters.

6.1. TRAVELING YESTERDAY AND TODAY

> The thing that hath been, it is that which shall be; and that which is done is that which shall be done: and there is no new thing under the sun. (Ecclesiastes 1:9)

This passage clearly indicates that what we are experiencing at the present time has already occurred in the past. In the same vein, the accidents that we see these days arrived in the past. The forces that provoked these accidents yesterday are those that manifest themselves today and will be those of tomorrow.

Beloved, there is nothing new under the sun. Technology and science did not exist in olden days. Nevertheless, men were traveling in the air, underneath water, and on earth as the following examples show:

-   IN THE AIR: Prior to our time, men were already traveling in the air. This was the case of Philip. As soon as he came out of the waters of baptism, the Spirit of God carried him from the desert to Azotus (Acts 8:39-40). In this day and age, it is not surprising to see people traveling by airplanes. And again, Elijah went up to heaven in a whirlwind caused by chariots and horses of fire. Of this ascension comes the principle of launching rockets into space (2 Kings 2:11).
-   UNDERNEATH THE WATER: Similarly, Jonah took a trip underneath the water in the belly of a fish, although there was no submarine in operation at that time. The sailors took Jonah and threw him into the sea. The Lord prepared a great fish to swallow Jonah and to vomit him three days later on the land (Jonah 2:1 and 10).
-   ON THE EARTH: The camels that brought Rebekah from Mesopotamia to Canaan (Genesis 24:61), the donkeys on which mounted the brothers of Joseph to go to Egypt (Genesis 42:25-27), and the chariots and the horses that Pharaoh used to chase the children of Israel (Exodus 14:9) are all symbols of transportation that we use today. These animals have participated in the moving of people from one place to another. Chariots pulled by horses at the time are the models of trains that we now have. Camels, because of their height and the long distance that they can travel, can symbolize the buses that we use. Considering its speed and courage, the horse symbolizes our sports cars.

While animals exercised their service toward men, they found themselves in accidents caused by spiritual forces. Nowadays, these phenomena still occur. The mortality rate caused by road accidents is very high. Not a week goes by where the media does not talk about road accidents. The security measures taken by the authorities have hardly reduced the rate of buffering in our cities. You can find license holders who do not want to drive because they are afraid of the dangers of the road, while others find themselves injured almost every month. If the people of this world understood that the forces of the spiritual world cause these calamities, I think we would have less road deaths. Let us go now in the scriptures to see how tragedies occurred in the days of the Gospels.

6.2. Disorder caused by God in the camp of the Egyptians

> And it came to pass, that in the morning watch the Lord looked unto the host of the Egyptians through the pillar of fire and of the cloud, and troubled the host of the Egyptians, And took off their chariot wheels, that they drave them heavily: so that the Egyptians said, Let us flee from the face of Israel; for the Lord fighteth for them against the Egyptians. (Exodus 14:24-25)

All night long, the Egyptians were pursuing the children of Israel with their horses and chariots, getting closer to them as they made their entrance into the Red Sea. In the morning watch, the Bible declares that the Lord, through the pillar of fire and of the cloud, troubled their host and took off their chariot wheels. While the Egyptians ran after the children of Israel, they did not see the pillar of fire and cloud that was between the two camps. God operated as a column of fire in the spiritual realm. However, the Egyptians were traveling at high speed on their chariots. Later, they saw the wheels of their chariots dismember from each other. God hindered their advancement.

Beloved, while you are traveling in your vehicle in the physical realm, the spirits in the spiritual realm are watching you in a similar way that God observed the camp of the Egyptians. Do you know that the spirits in the spiritual realm have the ability to touch objects that are in the physical world to the point of moving or rolling them? God in the spiritual realm was able to touch the wheels of the chariots and remove them. Here's what happens the moment demons want to cause accidents. While a vehicle is moving, these evil spirits will take off one of the wheels, disconnect the battery, unplug the cables, or loosen a mechanical part. This is why it is important for every driver to observe a moment of prayer on the wheels and mechanical parts of his vehicle before driving.

6.3. A SERPENT BY THE WAY

> Dan shall be a serpent by the way, an adder in the path, that biteth the horse heels, so that his rider shall fall backward. (Genesis 49:17)

This passage tells of a prophecy made by Jacob to his son, Dan, as well as on his offspring. Later, Moses picked up this prophecy on the tribe of the Danites:

> And of Dan he said, Dan is a lion's whelp: he shall leap from Bashan. (Deuteronomy 33:22)

From these two prophecies concerning the tribe of Dan, God announced that he would have come out of this tribe, heroes to deliver the people of Israel from the hand of their enemies.

The arrival of the famous Samson confirmed these prophecies (Judges 13:2-5). No security measures established by men, other than prayer, can prevent accidents provoked by demons. These accidents are caused by forces operating in the spiritual realm. These powers have the ability to see their victims while these do not see them. In Genesis 49:17, cited at the beginning of this chapter, the Lord outlines the activities of the world of darkness held against men on their path. The serpent placed on the road to cause the accident bites the horse so that as he falls, he overthrows the rider.

Here's how the agents of Satan operate to cause accidents. They throw occult objects (for example, wood, remains, or stones on the way of their victims). Once these preys cross this occult object, the demon attached thereto will cause a puncture that will bring to pass, thereafter, an accident. This is why you should always pray on the road you want to go through, in your going out and your coming in. This is intended both for drivers and pedestrians. Snakes, placed on the way, will wait for you to pass by to bite you.

6.4. HEART FAILURE

Many die behind the wheel of their vehicle even though they were not in a car accident. This is very common in our society. The causes of death are not always identified. Modern medicine diagnoses so often heart attacks.

Let us read what happened to King Ahab:

> And a certain man drew a bow at a venture, and smote the king of Israel between the joints of the harness: wherefore he said unto the driver of his

chariot, Turn thine hand, and carry me out of the
host; for I am wounded. And the battle increased
that day: and the king was stayed up in his chariot
against the Syrians, and died at even: and the blood
ran out of the wound into the midst of the chariot.
(1 Kings 22:34-35)

Three important elements should be drawn from these two
Bible verses. Firstly, an arrow came from the outside and hit
the king while he was in his chariot. Secondly, the king of Israel
found himself stuck in his chariot because of the intensity of the
fight. Thirdly, the king died while he was in his chariot.

Having said that, when you enter your vehicle, break the arrows
that fly through the air before starting your vehicle. Cover the
windows of your vehicle with the blood of Jesus so that the
arrows do not penetrate it. Ask the Holy Spirit to lock the doors
of your vehicle so that you may easily open them and get out in
case of problems.

Thou shalt not be afraid for the terror by night; nor
for the arrow that flieth by day. (Psalm 91:5)

In this biblical verse, the arrows that fly by day and that are not
visible to the naked eye are exposed. These arrows, from the
world of darkness, are thrown through the wind, the sun, and
the moon by the servants of Lucifer. These arrows are demons
flying through the air to destroy. They are the ones who cause
the death of drivers in their vehicles. By their power, they have
the ability to hold the vehicle's doors locked so that drivers may
not escape in an accident. We should not be afraid of them;
God had given us the power to trample over such things. In
the state of Virginia, located to the northeast side of the United

States, a man was driving when a tree fell on his car. He died on the spot.

6.5.   The Shipwrecks

> But the Lord sent out a great wind into the sea, and there was a mighty tempest in the sea, so that the ship was like to be broken. (Jonah 1:4)

At times shipwrecks are created by adverse weather conditions, sometimes they can be induced by spiritual forces. Some men who were traveling by boat went missing and were never found because of the powers of darkness, as demonstrated in the case of Jonah. The Lord kindled the storm that arose against the ship, which Jonah was on. On the contrary, in the boat where Jesus slept, the great storm that arose against the disciples was a work of the sea monster (Mark 4:37-39). In Psalm 74:13, King David honors the Lord for breaking the head of the dragons in the waters.

We can see that, accidents caused by demons, can affect all transportation systems: the land and sea routes as well as airlines and railroad tracks. Beloved, when traveling by boat or cruiser, pray that the breath of the mouth of the marine powers does not lift up from the waters a storm against you.

6.6.   Accidents caused by animals

> If an ox gore a man or a woman, that they die: then the ox shall be surely stoned, and his flesh shall not be eaten; but the owner of the ox shall be quit. (Exodus 21:28)

From time to time, the world of darkness uses animals to cause accidents. An ox, a buffalo, or a lion could attack a person while the latter is in the process of walking or riding a bicycle. God gave Moses the laws regarding animals that were to be presented to the people. The Lord pronounced the judgment to bring against an ox if it used its horns to strike a person (Exodus 21:28). We therefore find that accidents involving humans and animals had already been foreseen in God's timetable. Often, people who live in rural areas and farming areas are hit by animals. Sometimes these accidents come from sources that are not natural.

> And Aaron stretched out his hand over the waters of Egypt; and the frogs came up, and covered the land of Egypt. And the magicians did so with their enchantments, and brought up frogs upon the land of Egypt. (Exodus 8:6-7)

The frogs, which came up from the waters of Egypt, went to disturb the Egyptians in their home, in the street, and wherever they were. Their presence on the Egyptian territory was supernatural. These frogs were those that the Lord made to appear and those brought up by magicians. There are also some animals on earth that are not real animals. Some are spirits who have left the waters for the earth and that take the form of animals to cause accidents. In the book of Genesis 41:1-2 (NKJV), Pharaoh had a dream where he saw seven cows coming out of the river to the earth that started to eat grass. This practice used by the world of darkness allows these agents to cause the death of their victims without attracting any suspicion on them.

In conclusion, the sections of the prayers that follow will assist you to end the activities of spiritual forces through accidents.

Theses prayers will help you confound Satan and his kingdom by bringing against them an evil day.

6.7. PRAYER SECTION

1. Accidents that occurred yesterday will not take place in my life, in the name of Jesus.
2. The accidents that took place today, will not take place in my life, in the name of Jesus.
3. Any snake on my way, be crushed, in the name of Jesus.
4. Any adder on my path programmed against the wheels of my vehicle, I crush your head, in the name of Jesus.
5. By the heat of the sun, O Lord, destroy evil objects thrown on my way to cause accidents, in the name of Jesus.
6. I tear the eyes of evil spirits watching me while I'm driving, in the name of Jesus.
7. Any demon obstinate to mess up the vehicles that are at crossroads, be beaten with a rod, in the name of Jesus.
8. O Lord, fight for me against the spiritual forces while I'm driving, in the name of Jesus.
9. Angel of Satan that came to remove the wheels of my vehicle while I'm driving, be struck by thunder, in the name of Jesus.
10. Lord, put to flight the spirits who want to make my driving difficult, in the name of Jesus.
11. The streams of this country will not cover my vehicle, in the name of Jesus.
12. I order all astral hands outstretched against me while I drive to be dried, in the name of Jesus.
13. I command astral hands outstretched toward the sea of the country while I'm driving, to be covered with white leprosy, in the name of Jesus.

14. Any vehicle approaching me to cause an accident, move away by the power of God, in the name of Jesus.
15. I break the curse of voodoo and witchcraft thrown on my vehicle, in the name of Jesus.
16. Arrow causing death by accident thrown through the sun, the moon, and the wind while I'm driving, be broken, in the name of Jesus.
17. Any arrow flying by day or by night while I'm driving, go back to where you have come, in the name of Jesus.
18. My blood will not be spilled in a vehicle, in the name of Jesus.
19. Let the powers of darkness, who want to see my death at the wheel of my vehicle, be hanged, in the name of Jesus.
20. Power of Satan trying to keep me locked in my vehicle when I face danger, I sentence you to death, in the name of Jesus.
21. Lord, bring me out of accidents programmed against me by the kingdom of darkness, in the name of Jesus.
22. O Lord, while I drive, lead my vehicle, in the name of Jesus.
23. Whirlwind blown over the sea by the forces of darkness while I travel, be afflicted by the power of God, in the name of Jesus.
24. O Lord, calm the storms that rise on the sea while I am traveling by boat, in the name of Jesus.
25. Head of the sea monster threatening to sink my boat, be broken, in the name of Jesus.
26. Lord, lighten the vessel in which I travel on the waters, in the name of Jesus.
27. My affairs that are in this boat will not be thrown into the water, in the name of Jesus.
28. Any power drawing me against misfortunes while I travel by boat, be bitten by scorpions, in the name of Jesus.

29. Every vehicle coming from the waters and circulating in the streets, be destroyed by the east wind, in the name of Jesus.

30. Every spirit in human form driving in this city, be thrown into the everlasting fire, in the name of Jesus.

31. Divine fire, come down from heaven and burn the evil forces around my vehicle, in the name of Jesus.

32. Divine fire, come down from heaven and burn the evil protections that are in the vehicles of my enemies, in the name of Jesus.

33. Demon of fire sent to burn my vehicle, be fought by the angel of the Lord, in the name of Jesus.

34. Lord, deliver my vehicle from every satanic captivity, in the name of Jesus.

35. All oxen coming out of a stream to confront me on the road, be stoned, in the name of Jesus.

36. I break the horns of witchcraft cattle that came out of the forests to hit me, in the name of Jesus.

37. Every spirit that invades the body of an animal, using it to cause accidents, be dipped into mud, in the name of Jesus.

38. I consume the bones of the evil cattle walking against me, in the name of Jesus.

39. Lord, pierce with your arrows the head of the cattle that came out as a whirlwind to scatter me, in the name of Jesus.

40. There will be no more appearances of cattle on my path, in the name of Jesus.

6.8. PRAYER SECTION TO DO AFTER THE PURCHASE OR WHEN LOANING A USED VEHICLE

1. Confess: "Thou shalt also decree a thing, and it shall be established unto thee: and the light shall shine upon thy ways" (Job 22:28).

2. By the blood of Jesus, I erase the sins committed in this vehicle, in the name of Jesus.
3. By the blood of Jesus, I cancel the evil baths that have been made to purify this vehicle, in the name of Jesus.
4. I declare that the blood of men that sank in this vehicle will not fall upon my head, in the name of Jesus.
5. I declare that this vehicle will not be an instrument of destruction in the hands of Satan, in the name of Jesus.
6. I separate myself from all demonic activity in which this vehicle was involved, in the name of Jesus.
7. By the blood of Jesus, I destroy the smell of death that remained in this vehicle for having transported a deceased person, in the name of Jesus.
8. I bind every demon attached to this vehicle for *(choose from the list below)*, in the name of Jesus.

   - transporting members of occult groups
   - being used in bank robberies
   - carrying occult signs and images
   - killing an individual accidentally
   - being the property of a person belonging to a secret society
   - being stolen
   - being a subject of dispute between a dealer and the buyer
   - having chronic breakdowns

9. I reject all the problems that this vehicle caused to its former owners, in the name of Jesus.
10. By the blood of Jesus, I destroy the evil protection that was used on this vehicle, in the name of Jesus.

Please note: When finishing the prayers, you must anoint your vehicle with anointing oil as Jacob did on the stone, which he had took for his pillows (Genesis 28:18).

11. By the power of the Holy Spirit manifested in this anointing oil *(choose from the list below)*, in the name of Jesus.

   - I sanctify this vehicle, in the name of the Father, the Son, and the Holy Ghost
   - I separate this vehicle from all pollution and all impurity
   - I anoint the wheels, the motor, the connections, the cable, the windows, the doors, the lights, the mirrors, the seats, the steering wheel, and the brakes of this vehicle *(Join the action to the word by applying the oil on all the parts you mentioned)*.

Glorify the Lord once you have finished the prayer.

CHAPTER VII

ACCIDENTS CAUSED BY THE SPIRITUAL WORLD (PART 2)

In the second chapter on accidents caused by the spiritual world, we will study the case of Balaam the prophet, the son of Beor. We will look at precisely what happened to him during his journey to the land of Moab. The Lord Almighty would, by the story of this prophet, make us understand the hidden mysteries and weapons used by the enemy to afflict us. Beloved, seize the opportunity that God gives you through this revelation to be set free from darkness.

While they are at the wheel of their vehicle, drivers are often faced with difficult, mysterious, and sometimes inexplicable situations. The fact of driving for several years does not make anyone safe from accidents caused by the spiritual world. Only the power of God will be able to protect you against these accidents.

7.1. BALAAM'S DEPARTURE

And Balaam rose up in the morning, and saddled his ass, and went with the princes of Moab. And God's anger was kindled because he went: and the angel of the Lord stood in the way for an adversary against him. Now he was riding upon his ass, and his two servants were with him. And the ass saw the angel of the Lord standing in the way, and his sword drawn in his hand: and the ass turned aside out of the way, and went into the field: and Balaam smote the ass, to turn her into the way. But the angel of the Lord stood in a path of the vineyards, a wall being on this side, and a wall on that side. And when the ass saw the angel of the Lord, she thrust herself unto the wall, and crushed Balaam's foot against the wall: and he smote her again. And the angel of the Lord went further, and stood in a narrow place, where was no way to turn either to the right hand or to the left. And when the ass saw the angel of the Lord, she fell down under Balaam: and Balaam's anger was kindled, and he smote the ass with a staff. (Numbers 22:21-27)

In this story, Balaam rose up in the morning, saddled his ass, and went with the princes of Moab (Numbers 22:21). Balaam's attitude resembles that of some drivers. Before going on the road, they check the oil level, watch the water level in the tank, control the air in the tires, and heat the engine. This routine is observed in most vehicle owners. That is why it is written,

> And Balaam rose up in the morning, and saddled his ass. (Numbers 22:21a)

However, before leaving, Balaam failed to pray. This man had not submitted his journey into the hands of God. He had neither prayed for his donkey nor for those who were traveling with him. Many commit the same mistake as the prophet.

When they get up, they shower, dress quickly, and rush to their vehicle to go to work. Yet they are in error. They do not understand the Word of God and do not know its power.

> The sun shall not smite thee by day, nor the moon
> by night. (Psalm 121:6)

This scripture proves that the attacks of the world of darkness can be launched against a driver by day, through the sun, as well as by night, through the moon.

7.2.   THE ANGER OF GOD

In this section, we will observe the consequences of the anger of God through different parts of verses.

> And God's anger was kindled because he went.
> (Numbers 22:22a)

God was offended by the departure of Balaam with the princes of Moab. This trip irritated the Lord and made him angry. *Anger* is defined as follows:

> 1) A strong feeling of displeasure and usually of
> antagonism; 2) Rage. (*Merriam-Webster Online*, 2013)

In addition, Balaam did not know that this was creating trouble and that his departure angered God. Beloved, *anger* indicates the presence of a spirit or demon that, when it inhabits a person, places him in this state. God's anger was kindled against Balaam because he did not approve the decision of the prophet to travel with the princes of Moab. You know, beloved, that the spirits in the spiritual world can be angry against you by virtue of a decision you made, without you knowing it. You can decide to undertake some projects, such as buying a house, traveling, or getting married. That is why, before starting off anything at all, you must hurry to pray against the wrath of the forces that will be irritated against you in the spiritual world.

> And the angel of the Lord stood in the way for an adversary against him. (Numbers 22:22b)

The anger of God opposed to Balaam increased to the point where he sent his angel on the path of the prophet to hinder him. The angel was placed in front of the road on which the prophet traveled to prevent him to carry out this trip. This angel was operating in the spiritual realm and not the physical realm because angels have no material body.

> And the ass saw the angel of the Lord standing in the way, and his sword drawn in his hand: and the ass turned aside out of the way, and went into the field: and Balaam smote the ass, to turn her into the way. (Numbers 22:23)

Then the donkey that carried Balaam saw the angel who stood before her with a naked sword in his hand. God had opened the eyes of the ass to see what was happening in the spiritual world. The existence of the spiritual world is real. Beloved, what happens in this world may affect the life of an individual in the physical world. Balaam, who was riding on the ass in the physical realm, was unaware of what was taking place in the spiritual world. Prior to the presence of the angel of the Lord, it was the prophet who was leading the ass. This animal was moving according to the instructions of his master. Everything was going well between Balaam and his donkey until the angel appeared on the way. The control of the ass changed hands. The spiritual world had taken over.

> Balaam smote the ass, to turn her into the way. (Numbers 22:23c)

Once the eyes of the ass opened up and she saw the angel placed at the edge of the road, she turned away from her master's orders, taking the direction of the field. Balaam smote her in an attempt to reintegrate her on the road.

At this point, Balaam the prophet found himself in an accident, not knowing what was going on in the spiritual world. The ass on which was the guest of the king thrust herself unto the wall at the point where the feet of his master took a blow (Numbers 22:25). The fact that the ass turned away from its original path to the bush shows that the forces operating in the spiritual world have a great influence on objects, animals, and humans that are in the physical world.

The accident, which took place in the life of Balaam, is comparable to what drivers are experiencing on the road without understanding what happens to them. While these drivers find themselves at the steering wheel, some evil spirits, such as energies controlled by Luciferians, appear on their way to resist them and cause an accident. In addition, these demons, or these energies, will deviate the vehicle's circuit from the original path by the powers they possess, to an unknown direction, as a forest, ravine, or river, as was the case of the ass. At this point, drivers lose control of their vehicle. Their device is found to be under the influence of a demon. Their vehicle will no longer respond to the orders of the driver, as Balaam's ass no longer obeyed him.

In Numbers 22:26 we can understand other manifestation of this evil forces when they want to cause accident againts some drivers. They move in front of these people why they are driving. This is why we heard people say that they have seen ghost moving in front of them while they were driving or before they get into accident.

In conclusion, let us read the declarations of the angel of the Lord to Balaam after his eyes were opened.

> And the ass saw me, and turned from me these three times: unless she had turned from me, surely now also I had slain thee, and saved her alive. (Numbers 22:33)

This last statement of the angel to the prophet gives us clarification on certain circumstances that happen during accidents. At the moment when these powers are in the individual's way to resist him, they can kill a driver and damage his vehicle. In contrast, these forces can destroy the vehicle but leave the driver alive. They can take the life of the person against whom they were sent without reaching those traveling with him or her. The mission of the angel was against Balaam, but not against his servants or against the princes of Moab. So the angel acted only against this prophet. This revelation that the Bible gives us on Balaam's situation allows us to understand that spirits are often sent on the road specifically against drivers to resist them. This is why in some accidents only one person is killed. Often this is the only person that the world of darkness wanted to destroy.

In this story, the donkey saw the angel and turned away three times before him. Based on this fact, men found a way to protect their vehicle against accidents. As a result, these individuals resort to occult forces. The use of amulets (talismans), the rosary, the Bible (some people use the Bible as a fetish), and small coins are seen in several vehicles.

Table 7 compares what happened to Balaam when he was on his ass and what drivers can experience in a vehicle when they are attacked by the enemy.

Table 7:   Comparison between Balaam and his ass and drivers' experiences

Balaam and his ass	Drivers and their vehicle
Balaam mounted his ass without praying.	Drivers sit in their vehicle without praying.
God, who is in the spiritual world, was angry against Balaam because he was going to Moab. God sent his angel against him.	A spirit in the spiritual world may become irritated by a driver to the point of putting himself on his way to resist him. Spirits can be sent for the same cause on the path of an individual.
Balaam's efforts to bring his ass on the road were unsuccessful.	When the vehicle is under the control of spiritual forces, the steering wheel of the vehicle no longer obeys the instructions of the driver. His maneuvers are in vain. The vehicle will go on the opposite direction.
Balaam was unable to stop his ass. He had completely lost control of the ass.	Drivers find that the brakes no longer function. The vehicle will be totally under the control of the spiritual world, and the driver will be powerless in this situation, which will lead to panic.
The ass no longer met Balaam's orders.	The vehicle will follow the direction imposed by the force in the spiritual world.

Balaam and his ass	Drivers and their vehicle
The ass was no longer controlled by the physical world; the spiritual realm was now in charge of the ass. Now, the donkey replied to the orders given by the angel located on their path.	The driver shall find that a strange power deflected the vehicle from its original direction. At that particular moment, the driver can finish the race in a ravine, on a utility pole, or in a timber.
The mission of the angel of the Lord was against Balaam. The angel did nothing to the asses of Balaam's servants or of those of the princes of Moab.	When a spirit is sent to cause the death by accident of an individual, he will spare the lives of those who travel with him. In some cases, those traveling with the target can be killed.

Beloved, give up now any obscure protection used on your vehicle and return to the Lord. The prayers below will help you escape the forces that cause accidents. When the enemy shall rise against you, the power of the Lord will be your shadow.

7.3. Prayer section

1. I render powerless the power exercised over my vehicle by the forces in the spiritual world, in the name of Jesus.
2. I take authority over the automatic, mechanical, and electrical systems of this vehicle, in the name of Jesus.
3. I separate this vehicle of all contact with the spiritual world, in the name of Jesus.
4. I command the evil forces preventing the functions of this vehicle to respond to my maneuvers or my commands to withdraw themselves, in the name of Jesus.
5. Divine power, deflect from this vehicle the energies sent on my way through rituals or crystal balls, in the name of Jesus.
6. I reverse the control exercised over this vehicle by the beings in the spiritual world, in the name of Jesus.

7. I declare that this vehicle is delivered from the activities of the spiritual world, in the name of Jesus.

8. I contest and reject the orders and the directions given to my vehicle by the forces in the spiritual world, in the name of Jesus.

9. Every spirit in the spiritual world rising to divert this vehicle from its original path, be devoured by worms, in the name of Jesus.

10. By the power of God, I submit this vehicle under my authority, and I declare that its functions will respond to the orders I will give to it, in the name of Jesus.

11. During the day, the sun shall not smite my vehicle nor the moon by night, in the name of Jesus.

12. Let the anger of the spirit ignited against me while I'm driving destroy them, in the name of Jesus.

13. I put to pieces the angels of Satan, offended by the fact that I am driving this vehicle, in the name of Jesus.

14. Cursed be the wrath of strange gods rising against me while I drive, in the name of Jesus.

15. Angel of Satan sent on my way to resist me, bend down and I will pass, in the name of Jesus.

16. I run over the evil spirits placed on my way to resist me in the name of Jesus.

17. Today, I cover this vehicle by the shadow of the hand of God, in the name of Jesus.

18. Lord, let me know the hidden things I do not know about this vehicle, in the name of Jesus.

19. Any demon placed on my way of departure to withstand this vehicle, be covered with lice, in the name of Jesus.

20. Any demon placed on my way of return to withstand this vehicle, be covered with dust, in the name of Jesus.

21. Any instrument of death in the hands of the spirit placed on my path, fall and be broken, in the name of Jesus.

22. I chain the angels of death placed on the path of my vehicle to kill me, in the name of Jesus.

23. Angel of death moving in front of my vehicle, wherever it goes, be confused, in the name of Jesus.

24. My vehicle, receive the power to run over the energies controlled by crystal balls or satanic agents, in the name of Jesus.

25. While I drive, every human spirit that comes to overthrow my vehicle, lick up the grass like an ox, in the name of Jesus.

26. Let the evil spirit that has seized the steering wheel of my vehicle to create a collision be thrown to the lake of fire, in the name of Jesus.

27. My bones will not be broken in an accident, in the name of Jesus.

28. My flesh will not be torn, burned, or destroyed in an accident, in the name of Jesus.

29. The members of my body will not be separated or torn to pieces in an accident, in the name of Jesus.

30. Any ritual that has been done to protect this vehicle against accidents, receive double destruction, in the name of Jesus.

31. I bring destruction unto any talismans, rosaries, and small coins that have been used in this vehicle to protect it, in the name of Jesus.

32. Lord, take away from this vehicle the evil caused by the use of occult objects, in the name of Jesus.

33. I apply the blood of Jesus against the evils forces introduced into this vehicle to protect it, in the name of Jesus.

34. My legs will not be broken in an accident, in the name of Jesus.

35. Any demon programmed to stop my vehicle in the middle of the road while I am driving, be swallowed by the ground, in the name of Jesus.

36. My blood will not spill in my vehicle, in the name of Jesus.
37. Death will not locate me in my vehicle, in the name of Jesus.
38. The evil tree of this city will not fall over my vehicle while I'm driving, in the name of Jesus.
39. I will not die on the wheel of this vehicle, in the name of Jesus.

CHAPTER VIII

BAD NEWS

B efore consulting the Holy Scriptures to see how bad news has affected the lives of some individuals, I would like to recount to you what happened to a man during a business trip. This man, who earned his living by importing and exporting, left the Central African Republic to go to Cameroon in order to purchase goods. On his way back, he received a phone call from his wife. While she was explaining to him how a dog had bitten one of their children, this businessman fell down and died.

Beloved, close your eyes and pray, "Any bad news that wants to take me away from the land of the living, receive your destruction, in the name of Jesus."

Now let us examine different reactions of biblical characters, following the delivering of bad news: Job, Eli, his daughter-in-law, and King David.

8.1. JOB'S CASE

> And there was a day when his sons and his daughters
> were eating and drinking wine in their eldest
> brother's house: And there came a messenger unto
> Job, and said, The oxen were plowing, and the asses
> feeding beside them: And the Sabeans fell upon
> them, and took them away; yea, they have slain
> the servants with the edge of the sword; and I only
> am escaped alone to tell thee. While he was yet
> speaking, there came also another, and said, The fire
> of God is fallen from heaven, and hath burned up
> the sheep, and the servants, and consumed them;
> and I only am escaped alone to tell thee. While he
> was yet speaking, there came also another, and said,
> The Chaldeans made out three bands, and fell upon
> the camels, and have carried them away, yea, and
> slain the servants with the edge of the sword; and I
> only am escaped alone to tell thee. While he was yet
> speaking, there came also another, and said, Thy sons
> and thy daughters were eating and drinking wine in
> their eldest brother's house: And, behold, there came
> a great wind from the wilderness, and smote the
> four corners of the house, and it fell upon the young
> men, and they are dead; and I only am escaped alone
> to tell thee. Then Job arose, and rent his mantle, and
> shaved his head, and fell down upon the ground, and
> worshipped. (Job 1:13-20)

In a single day, a succession of horrible news disturbed the life
of Job. As his ears would hear of a misfortune, another one
would come. In this bad day, Job's destiny rocked from the best

to the worst. The empire he had spent so many years to build collapsed at once. In a twinkling of an eye, all his work and effort went up in smoke. A difficult time debuted in the life of Job.

Among the inhabitants of this world, there are some that live under the influence of bad news for days, weeks, months, and even years. These events bring a devastating change in their lives. From the joy they had, they find themselves in trouble. From the peace they enjoyed, they are confronted with problems. They go from hope to despair, from abundance to shortage.

8.1.1. Job rented his mantle

After hearing these bad news, Job rented the *mantle* that he wore over his clothes. However, he did not expose his nakedness or the sensitive parts of his body.

By definition, a *mantle* is

> A loose sleeveless garment worn over other clothes: cloak. (*Merriam-Webster Online*, 2013)

Terrorized by the bad news, he kept himself from acting unrighteous in the sight of the Lord. In this day and age, the show offered by Job by tearing his clothes is common. Often, beings expose their nakedness because they have heard evil tidings. The delivery of bad news leads to humiliation and shame in the lives of these people. Some will put their hands to their heads or will cover their faces to cry. Others will seek to throw themselves from skyscrapers or make unsafe practices for their lives.

8.1.2. Job shaved his head

Thereafter, Job shaved his head. Disturbing news can push an individual to take violent acts that will destroy their own body. The individual acts against his soul, under the influence of unpleasant news. Job took a tool to shave his head. Also, you will see some people pulling their hair or banging their head to react to a disaster.

8.1.3. Job fell down upon the ground and worshipped

Finally, in these moments of pain, Job threw himself on the ground as a sign of abandonment into the hands of the Lord. Generally, when some people hear bad news, they fall and roll on the ground, screaming like animals. Job was able to master the circumstance. Once on the ground, he bowed down before the God of Abraham to plead his cause. This man had prevailed over the situation. Job entered directly in prayer and sought the face of God to understand what was happening. In this event, Job did not accuse anybody nor did he go complain to any individual. This gesture proves that Job was resisting adversity.

Beloved, the last time you heard negative news, did you immediately go into prayer? Are you one of those who let themselves be knocked over by bad news? Do you consult strange gods after hearing disastrous news? The lesson we draw from this last act of Job is as follows: in misfortunes, he did not put himself in his Adam's outfit while he prostrated before the Lord.

Now, deceitful workers transforming themselves into apostles of Christ have infiltrated false doctrines in the church. They teach the sheep the need to undress to plead their case before the Lord in difficult times. Most often, pastors quote the example of Job. Some of these ministers in their sanctuary find themselves praying on their sheep while they are fully undressed. Are they not crucifying the Gospel by doing so? What gods do these shepherds serve? We are saddened to hear our sisters talk about the experience they have underwent at the hands of false pastors. In addition, some recount how they prayed naked in their home or outside, late at night. What pleasure does God have to see their nakedness? Aren't those who do this sort of prayers and the ministers who advise them confused? These workers of iniquity with hungry bellies pollute our churches. Their end will be according to their works.

8.2.   Prophet Eli's case

> And the messenger answered and said, Israel is fled before the Philistines, and there hath been also a great slaughter among the people, and thy two sons also, Hophni and Phinehas, are dead, and the ark of God is taken. And it came to pass, when he made mention of the ark of God, that he fell from off the seat backward by the side of the gate, and his neck brake, and he died: for he was an old man, and heavy. And he had judged Israel forty years. (1 Samuel 4:17-18)

Eli was the priest of the Lord in Israel for almost forty years. His function allowed him to keep the ark of the Lord in the temple. During the war between the people of Israel and the Philistines, the Israelites were defeated in battle. The elders requested that the ark of God be carried on the conflict zone so that God would deliver them from their enemies. The sons of the priest Eli brought the ark to the place of conflict (1 Samuel

4: 3-4). The battle was to the advantage of the Philistines, and the ark had been torn from the hands of the Israelites. Finally, one soldier escaped from the battlefield to bring the bad news in the city and to the priest.

That day, Prophet Eli received a set of bad news: the destruction of his two children and the defeat of Israel. But these bad news did not take away the life of the priest. In short, the notification of the taking of the ark of the covenant was the cause of his death.

Eli was old, blind, and overweight. However, he suffered no life-threatening illnesses. His death did not come following an altercation, an accident, a blast from firearm or poisoning. When his ears heard of the taking of the ark, he fell from the siege where he sat and broke his neck.

8.3.   Eli's daughter-in-law's case

> And his daughter in law, Phinehas' wife, was with child, near to be delivered: and when she heard the tidings that the ark of God was taken, and that her father in law and her husband were dead, she bowed herself and travailed; for her pains came upon her. (1 Samuel 4:19)

After reading this, note that bad news can precipitate the occurrence of an event in the life of a person. Thus, a woman may have a miscarriage, or see her menstrual cycle be triggered, from the communication of these news. Thus, the delivery of the daughter-in-law of Prophet Eli was precipitated following the announcement of the horror that struck her family-in-law. Her contractions forced her to bend, and she gave birth to her child, who was born the same day that his father, grandfather and uncle died. Hence, the day of joy of this lady was turned into sorrow by the enemy.

8.4. KING DAVID'S CASE

King Saul was chasing the young David and his troops in the mountains (1 Samuel 23:26-28). Saul wanted, at all costs, the death of the young David. The king opposed his accession to the throne, preferring to place there his son Jonathan (1 Samuel 20:30-31). To deliver David and his troops from their pursuers, God did not send angels or bring down stones from heaven. The Lord had hardly prevented the gruesome plan of Saul. The Mighty One of Jacob looked down from heaven at Saul's act, knowing how he would proceed to take David out of this situation. Saul was about to lay hands on David and his troops, when a *messenger* came to announce bad news. From that moment, Saul returned from pursuing after David and went against the Philistines. Once again, God acted miraculously by saving the life of the young David.

The Lord is the master of the times and the seasons. Have faith in God. David's case demonstrates that bad news is used by the powers in the spiritual world as a weapon of *deliverance* or destruction. Now let us look at how the spiritual worlds operate from this tool.

8.5. THE POWER THAT OPERATES THROUGH BAD NEWS

Certainly, men do not die from hearing bad news or because they threw themselves violently on the ground or did something stupid. By carefully reading the case of the priest Eli, you'll wonder how his death came. This man was sitting on a seat. How did he fall backward and break his neck? The fall of the priest was strange. The spiritual world was involved in his death. God had revealed to Samuel that he would bring judgment against the house of Eli. What had really happened on the day of the death of this priest?

> Surely I will send a spirit upon him, and he shall hear a rumor and return to his own land; and I will cause him to fall by the sword in his own land. (2 Kings 19:7, NKJV)

In this passage, God speaks to the prophet Isaiah of his decision to arrest the king of Assyria, who came to invade the kingdom of Judah. God announces that he will put in this monarch a spirit and that, when he hears a rumor, will flee to his country and perish. First of all, note that God had to delegate a power against the king of Assyria before he receives the news. The mission of the spirit sent against the king was to put him on the run when he would hear to the bad news. So we can conclude that there is a force acting through the bad news.

In the same vein, a similar phenomenon happened to the priest Eli. A spirit had been sent against him to finish him off when he was going to learn of the taking of the ark of Israel. The minute his ears heard this bad news, this spirit threw him from his seat to the back, and he broke his neck.

Beloved, when a judgment of death through bad news is directed in opposition to an individual in the world of darkness, a spirit of death is sent to execute the judgment against that person. The action of this spirit will take effect precisely when the terrible information will be proclaimed to the victim. This is how some people die the minute they are told sad news.

When you have to tell someone bad news, do not be like those who want to know if the person is standing or lying prior to talking to them about the misfortune. If their interlocutor is standing, they will ask him to sit down because of the hard news to be published. Will you carry on your conscience the death of an individual for having notified him of an event that would have snatched him from the face of the earth? Prior to sharing some sad news, pray against the forces acting through bad news. In this way, the person who learns this misfortune will be protected.

8.6. Prayer section

1. Lord, protect my ears from bad news, in the name of Jesus.
2. Lord, deliver my life from the power of bad news, in the name of Jesus.
3. O Lord, this year arise and destroy bad news, in the name of Jesus.
4. Powers of bad news, throw yourselves on the ground, in the name of Jesus.
5. I knock down the powers that are behind bad news, in the name of Jesus.
6. Upon the announcement of bad news, my mouth will not place a judgment against me, in the name of Jesus.
7. Upon the announcement of bad news, my hands will not rise against me, in the name of Jesus.
8. I cancel any bowing before foreign gods at the communication of bad news, in the name of Jesus.
9. My hair will not fall to the ground under the influence of bad news, in the name of Jesus.
10. I punish any bad news that would *(choose from the list below)*, in the name of Jesus.

    -   compel me to expose my nakedness

- force me to commit crimes
- make me odious in the eyes of men
- put me in a great anger

10. I put to flight the spirits of death attached to bad news, in the name of Jesus.
11. Let the mind of the spirits planning to knock me down after the publication of bad news be covered by worms, in the name of Jesus.
12. After the announcement of bad news, my neck will not be broken, in the name of Jesus.
13. I break the head of the spirit assigned to kill me after the notification of bad news, in the name of Jesus.
14. I wipe out the pain programmed on my body as a result of bad news, in the name of Jesus.
15. I pass to the sword anxiety and fear caused by bad news, in the name of Jesus.
16. Lord, trouble the wrath of men who rise against me in the declaration of bad news, in the name of Jesus.
17. Lord, through bad news, take away all them that persecute me, in the name of Jesus.
18. Messenger of bad news, be visited by the Lord, in the name of Jesus.
19. Through bad news, I escape from the hands of those pursuing me, in the name of Jesus.
20. Let the ears of the forces who want to hear the bad news from me, become dizzy, in the name of Jesus.
21. I break the chain of bad news prepared against me and my family, in the name of Jesus.
22. Mighty One of Jacob, destroy the forces of bad news placed in ambush against me, in the name of Jesus.
23. Mighty One of Jacob, shake the voice of bad news, in the name of Jesus.

24. I escape the accidents caused by bad news, in the name of Jesus.
25. Let the spirits of precipitation that manifest themselves with the publication of bad news be thrown into the pit, in the name of Jesus.
26. All forecasts of bad news about my life, drift off, in the name of Jesus.
27. Any demon programmed inside me, waiting for the proclamation of bad news to manifest, jump out and go to a dry place, in the name of Jesus.
28. I receive the divine power to escape danger, in the name of Jesus.

CHAPTER IX

NOSTRILS' DELIVERANCE

Our teaching will be based on the various evil activities undertaken against man through his nostrils, as they are denounced in the Word of God. Then we will cry out to the Lord in the section of aggressive prayers so that he frees us.

9.1. BREATHING: A VITAL ACTIVITY

During the Creation, the Lord formed man out of the dust of the ground. The latter became a living soul when the Creator breathed into his nostrils the breath of life (Genesis 2:7). Nostrils, like all other parts of the body, are of great importance to human beings. In fact, we must watch our nostrils carefully. It is possible to meet a person who is blind, deaf, dumb, or unable to walk. Nevertheless, he may well be alive. Beloved, is there on earth a human being who lives without breathing? Impossible. This is why the devil can attack our nostrils as well as he can assault other organs of our body.

In this context, the biblical story that relates to this phenomenon is that of the apostle Paul. One day, Paul stood on the island of Melita. There, a viper fastened on his hand when he gathered a bundle of sticks. The apostle Paul shook the venomous beast into the fire and freed his hand from the grip of the snake. This was a great deliverance (Acts 28:3-5).

As Paul did for his hand, we must shake off these evil strangers occupying our nostrils, to free ourselves from their control.

The word *deliverance* signifies

> the state of being saved from something dangerous or unpleasant. Liberation, rescue. (*Merriam-Webster Online*, 2013)

At present, let us verify what the scriptures indicate on activities carried out against our nostrils. The different attacks of the evil one against nostrils have been classified into six categories.

9.2.   FIRST CATEGORY: LACK OF SMELL

Psalm 115:6 declares, "They have ears, but they hear not: noses have they, but they smell not." In this passage, the Bible refers to handmade idols, revered and worshiped by humans. The psalmist indicates that such idols have a lack of *smell* despite them having a *nose*. A *nose* is defined as follows:

> 1) The part of the face that bears the nostrils and covers the anterior part of the nasal cavity; broadly: this part together with the nasal cavity; 2) The sense of smell; 3) The vertebrate olfactory organ. (*Merriam-Webster Online*, 2013)

That said, our nostrils are used, among other things, to breathe. They are also present to smell natural odors. Humans have five senses: sight for the eyes, hearing for the ears, touch for the skin, taste for tongue, and *smell* for the nose. *Smell* is defined as follows:

> 1) To perceive the odor or scent of through stimuli affecting the olfactory nerves: get the odor or scent of with the nose; 2) To detect or become aware of as if by the sense of smell. (*Merriam-Webster Online*, 2013)

All humans breathe through the nose. Yet some hardly perceive natural odors. As soon as the Mighty One of Jacob made this statement about the idols through his servant David, the devil quickly found a weapon to use against humans. Let us read what Paul wrote to the Corinthians:

> And lest I should be exalted above measure through the abundance of the revelations, there was given to me a thorn in the flesh, the messenger of Satan to buffet me, lest I should be exalted above measure. (2 Corinthians 12:7)

The word *messenger* means

> One who bears a message or does an errand. (*Merriam-Webster Online*, 2013)

Only two categories of beings can carry Satan's messages: a demon or his agent, meaning witches and wizards. According to Apostle Paul, the devil had placed a demon in his *flesh*. This demon is a *messenger* of Satan. Now, we understand that Paul was referring to a demon placed inside his physical body to buffet him. He was not talking about a physical person.

A French translation of this scripture, the Louis Segond (LSG) version, makes it clear because the expression used is angel of Satan rather than messenger:

> Et pour que je ne sois pas enflé d'orgueil, à cause de l'excellence de ces révélations, il m'a été mis une écharde dans la chair, un ange de Satan pour me souffleter et m'empêcher de m'enorgueillir. (2 Corinthians 12:7, LSG)

The *flesh* is defined as follows:

> 1) The soft parts of the body of an animal and especially of a vertebrate; especially: the parts composed chiefly of skeletal muscle as distinguished from internal organs, bone, and integument; 2) The physical nature of human beings. (*Merriam-Webster Online*, 2013)

This demon programmed into Paul's flesh gave him blows to prevent him from becoming proud. Here is why you find people who are discerning increasingly less natural fragrances. Satan has placed a demon in the receivers of their nasal cavity to prevent them from perceiving natural aromas.

9.3. SECOND CATEGORY: SUPERNATURAL SMELL

> I have sent among you the pestilence after the manner of Egypt: your young men have I slain with the sword, and have taken away your horses; and I have made the stink of your camps to come up unto your nostrils: yet have ye not returned unto me, saith the Lord. (Amos 4:10)

In this verse, God speaks to the children of Israel. The Lord made it clear to his people that he is responsible for the various ailments they passed through.

God is a power that blesses and forgives sins. However, from time to time, the Lord can turn against you by causing death, famine, and affliction. The devil is not always the one who is at the source of your difficulties. The Creator will become your enemy when your ways are unpleasant to him. In the case of the children of Israel, the Almighty is the one who brought up to their nostrils pollution from their camp. The epidemic or plague of stench suffered by the children of Israel were not due to poor hygiene conditions or unsafe or dumped toxic waste in their environment. It was the result of an unpleasant smell produced by God. The Lord carried the smell of feces, urine, trash cans, dead animals, and dirty water toward the nostrils of the children of Israel.

In Leviticus 26:31, the Lord said unto the children of Israel that he will no longer smell the savor of their sweet odors. This scripture shows that spirits have nostrils that allow them to smell. Therefore, they can tell the difference between a good or bad smell.

These odors did not spread in the air, as it was the case of which Joel refers here:

> I will drive the northern horde far from you, pushing it into a parched and barren land; its eastern ranks will drown in the Dead Sea and its western ranks in the Mediterranean Sea. And its stench will go up; its smell will rise. Surely he has done great things! (Joel 2:20, NIV)

What happened to the children of Israel was supernatural. Regardless of the measures they took to clean and scent their camps, the stench was still evident in their nostrils. Beloved, as God did it against the people of Israel, the demons do the same against their victims. Unclean spirits have the ability to reproduce the smell of feces in the nostrils of an individual. The latter will be the only one to inhale the smell. Those around him will hardly smell these stenches. Demons can spread bad odors in the air, in a home, or in an environment. When a person can smell the exhalations that others around him cannot naturally perceive, his olfactory system is under the influence and control of a demon. His nostrils, therefore, need to be delivered. In contrast, some people inhale good odors. This, in no way, determines the presence of angels. The devil is usually the cause of these good smells, whose purpose is to deceive his victims.

9.4. THIRD CATEGORY: NOSE BLEEDING

Nasal bleeding is one of the methods used by our enemy to torment those against whom he has extended his hand. Beloved, Satan systematically copies the works of the Lord. He artificially reproduces the activities that Jehovah made or reported in his Word. The Bible tells us to be imitators of God (Ephesians 5:1, NKJV). Well, the dragon became a plagiarist of the works of the Holy of Holies. Whenever you are under the effects of a particular attack, see the scriptures about it.

In the Bible, the Holy Spirit has solved the case of bleeding, such as the situation of the woman who bled for twelve years (Luke 8:43-46). The doctors lost all hope of treating this woman, because her problem emanated from the spiritual realm. This illness was an activity of demons. It is the same for a certain category of people who suffer from blood flows through the nostrils. Only the power of Jesus can heal them. To be treated, these patients must touch the garment of Christ, as did the woman who was bleeding.

Now, let us analyze this proverb:

> For as churning cream produces butter, and as twisting the nose produces blood, so stirring up anger produces strife. (Proverbs 30:33, NIV)

This Bible verse indicates that blood could flow from the nostrils by the pressure or twisting exerted on them. The verb *twist* signifies the following:

> 1) To alter the meaning of; 2) To pull off, turn, or break by torsion. (*Merriam-Webster Online*, 2013)

The verb to *turn* means the following:

> 1) To cause to move around an axis or a center: make rotate or revolve; 2) To bend or change the course of. (*Merriam-Webster Online*, 2013)

In fact, the blood flows from the heart to the organs through the arteries. Thus, from the vessels, the demons can cause the blood to go out of the nostrils of the victim by twisting his nose.

9.5. Fourth category: smoke from the nose

The psalmist wrote:

> There went up a smoke out of his nostrils, and fire out of his mouth devoured: coals were kindled by it. (Psalm 18:8)

Indeed, the nostrils of God were up in smoke for two reasons. Firstly, he was irritated to see his anointed David in danger. Secondly, it was because of the presence of fire in his mouth. Above all, it is absolutely necessary to have fire for smoke to come out! Indeed, the adage says, "There is no smoke without fire." The fire and smoke coming out of the mouth and nostrils of God were intended to bring deliverance in the life of David because he was at risk.

That said, the creation of the cigar, cigarette, joint, or pipe comes from the world of darkness. This idea originates from Satan, the prince of the power of the air. The action of those who engage in tobacco corresponds to the details of what happens in Psalm 18:8. This act took place in the spiritual realm and was revealed to David by the Holy Spirit. Fire gushed from the mouth of the Lord. At the same time, smoke emerged from his nostrils. If you pay attention to a being who smokes, you will find that before seeing the smoke out of his nostrils, he must light tobacco, using a lighter or a match. The fire will remain permanently on the cigarette that is located in the smoker's mouth. The latter will suck the smoke, which is then exhaled through his nostrils. The fire burning on the cigarette, placed in the mouth of the smoker, contributes to his destruction.

However, these smokers do not exhale smoke out of their nostrils because they are irritated. It is rather a manifestation of the works of the flesh. The desire to smoke is controlled in the lives of these beings by the demon that is in their nostrils. From the moment the finger of the Lord drives out that spirit of their noses, they will be delivered from the desire to inhale puffs of tobacco forever.

Still, some ask where the Bible forbids cigarette smoking. They ask this question because they ignore the tricks of the devil.

Satan is the architect and founder of the cigar and all the works of the flesh described in Galatians 5:19-21. In this passage, the Bible speaks of "such like": smoking is one of those things. When the devil saw the Lord in his anger spouting fire from his mouth, and from his nostrils, smoke, Satan released David from the bonds in which he kept him. In trickery, the serpent got the idea to bring living beings to evacuate smoke from their nostrils. Thus, he urged man to create a cigar, cigarette, calumet, and all that can be smoked. Beloved, all smokers glorify Satan for the destruction of their souls.

9.6.   FIFTH CATEGORY: SNORING

In the following verse, Job speaks first of his breathing and then of the breath of God present in his nostrils:

> All the while my breath is in me, and the spirit of God is in my nostrils. My lips shall not speak wickedness, nor my tongue utter deceit. (Job 27:3-4)

Right here, Job's nostrils were anointed by the power of the Lord, as it was the case of the prophet Isaiah when he was visited by the angel of God, a seraphim (Isaiah 6:6-7). The presence of the breath of God in the nostrils of Job allowed him not to sin with his lips or tongue. In truth, a person may have in him breath and lack the presence of God's spirit in his nostrils. The absence of divine breath in a person will lead him to sin with his lips or his tongue. Job's nostrils were no more ordinary; they had just received the divine touch.

Beloved, the nostrils of an individual can carry a spirit that comes from God or the devil, as we have seen in the case of Job. The presence of the spirit of Satan in the nose of an individual will lead him to sin on one hand and will not prevent him from breathing on the other hand. This evil spirit will snuggle into the nostrils of his victim for other missions that he will run whenever the opportunity presents itself to him.

At present, let us read what Psalm 18:15 declares,

> Then the channels of waters were seen, and the foundations of the world were discovered at thy rebuke, O Lord, at the blast of the breath of thy nostrils.

The word *blast* means

> A violent gust of wind. (*Merriam-Webster Online*, 2013)

As for *gust*, it is defined as follows:

> 1) A sudden brief rush of wind; 2) A sudden outburst: surge. (*Merriam-Webster Online*, 2013)

When the Lord came to deliver his servant David from the hands of his enemies, great manifestations were held in these moments of liberation. By the revelation obtained through the Holy Spirit, the psalmist declares that it was by the sound of the breath of the Lord's nostrils that the channels of waters and the foundations of the world were discovered. This noise occurred when the breath of God was out of his nostrils. The breath of God, which came out of his nostrils, represented his power or his Holy Spirit. We can conclude that an unclean spirit can produce sounds, either inside or outside of an individual (Jeremiah 6:7, NIV).

In the case of Job, the Holy Spirit in his nostrils allowed him to move away from sin. In the case of God, the breath of his nostrils produced sounds out of them. So Satan programs demons in human nostrils to generate sound. What we know as snoring occurs when people are asleep and varies from one person to another. The enemy wants to create a nuance or confusion by making men believe that it is by inhaling during sleep that these sounds are produced. This statement is false. Why don't men snore while they are awake? Aren't they breathing? When a person breathes, the demon into his nostrils directly emits sounds or noise at the same pace as his breath. When he inspires, the demon stops his activities. Snoring manifested in the nostrils of the people in their sleep indicate the presence of evil spirits in the nose of the latter. As a result, their nostrils require deliverance.

These days, this demonic chain retains many in the church whether they are ministers or pastors. But some deliverance ministers claim to release people that evil spirits torment. These ministers are unaware that they are themselves demonized. Around 2005, I attended a Christian conference that took place in Jacksonville, in the state of Florida in the United States. The seminar was organized by Pastor Gwen R. Shaw, author of the book *Day by Day*.[2] Different members of spiritual warfare ministries were present at this seminar. Some pastors were referred to as powerful deliverance ministers. Because they were from other continents, these men of God, who came especially for the seminar, found themselves faced with jet lag. So they began to sleep during the conference. During the seminar, participants were greatly disturbed by noises from snoring of one of these deliverance ministers savoring his sleep without any

---

2   Gwen R. Shaw, *Day by Day: A Daily Praise Offering (Heavenly Truths as Given by the Holy Spirit to Gwen R. Shaw).* (Engeltal Press: 1987), 469 pages.

worry. It was in vain that his partner woke him up. Sometime later, he fell back in his sleep, and snoring resumed.

Some homes have been broken because of snoring. Husbands and wives avoid sleeping near one another because their rest is disturbed. Medicine, despite all research efforts, still gives lousy and ineffective results against snoring. Gadgets offered to patients to reduce noise when sleeping provide no solution. This activity is a spiritual one. Only Jesus Christ has the solution. That is why the Word says,

> When thou liest down, thou shalt not be afraid: yea, thou shalt lie down, and thy sleep shall be sweet. (Proverbs 3:24)

9.7.   SIXTH CATEGORY: PREDICTING BY NOSTRILS

The following passage refers to the horse, which, through his nostrils, has the ability to smell the battle from far off, the thunder of the captains, and the shouting.

> At the blast of the trumpet he says, "Aha!" He smells the battle from afar, The thunder of captains and shouting. (Job 39:25, NKJV)

From the definition of the word *smell* found in section 9.2, we understand that the horse can, through his nose, discern an event, a noise, or a smell from afar. Animals have abilities that distinguish them from human beings. From the moment people hold qualities possessed by animals, there is a problem. Unclean spirits lodged in the nostrils of some people give to them the same ability possessed by animals. These people use their nostrils to discern, divine, or discover by the odor. To cite a few examples, the demons attached to their nose can inform them of the arrival of a vehicle in a distance from the sound of its engine, the arrival of an individual through his body odor, a fire that occurred in another location through the burning smell, or even words of a conversation that is taking place in a different location.

Beloved, let us pay attention to the manifestations of spiritual gifts in ourselves and in others. Satan manipulates humans. When these skills are manifested in you, try to find out their sources. Today, Satan uses the nostrils of many Christians to express his power. These nostrils need to be delivered from evil invaders. The prayers below will help us to resist these forces so that they will move away from us.

9.8. PRAYER SECTION

1. I cast out of my respiratory system the deposits of unclean spirits, in the name of Jesus.
2. Breath of the forces of darkness polluting my respiratory system, be neutralized, in the name of Jesus.
3. Any spirit blowing in my nostrils, be beaten by the storm, in the name of Jesus.
4. Angel of Satan preventing my sense of smell to perceive natural smell, be carried away by the winds, in the name of Jesus.
5. I break the curse of destruction pronounced against my nostrils, in the name of Jesus.
6. I break the nose of idols and evil statuettes, in the name of Jesus.
7. I humiliate the power of the mouths declaring that although I have a nose, I will not smell, in the name of Jesus.

8. Evil spirit that is carrying to my nose infections of this environment, be destroyed by fire, in the name of Jesus.

9. Right hand of the Lord, destroy the evil spirits who are spreading smells in the air, in the name of Jesus.

10. Deliver my nostrils, Lord, and they shall be delivered, in the name of Jesus.

11. By the blood of Jesus, I move away infections of this environment that mounted on my nostrils, in the name of Jesus.

12. Every unclean spirit in my veins, pushing the blood out of my nose, get thee behind me, in the name of Jesus.

13. All demons squeezing my nose to produce blood, I break your head, in the name of Jesus.

14. Lord, fortify my nose for it to resist the pressure of the forces of darkness, in the name of Jesus.

15. Divine power, stop the flow of blood in my nostrils, in the name of Jesus.

16. My sense of smell, be released from the power of the dog, in the name of Jesus.

17. Any evil ability to divine, discern, and predict manifested in my sense of smell, be destroyed, in the name of Jesus.

18. Separate me, Lord, from the powers giving me the ability to divine through my sense of smell, in the name of Jesus.

19. All power in my nostrils giving me the ability to sense from far away an event, noise, or conversation, be chased away, in the name of Jesus.

20. I bring the wrath of God against the spirits producing sounds in my nostrils when I sleep, in the name of Jesus.

21. I silence the spirits that make noise in my nostrils, in the name of Jesus.

22. Let the breath of my nostrils be released from every demonic noise, in the name of Jesus.

23. Noise of the breath of unclean spirits in my nostrils, perish, in the name of Jesus.

24. I disgrace the snoring spirits who plan to humiliate me in public, in the name of Jesus.

25. As long as I will have my breath, the breath of Satan will not exist in my nostrils, in the name of Jesus.

26. Every spirit lifting up smoke in my nostrils, go into the bottomless pit, in the name of Jesus.

27. Anything in my nostrils, like smoke, be torn away, in the name of Jesus.

28. Let every serpent in my nostrils be crushed, in the name of Jesus.

29. I pull out of my nose the buckle of the world of darkness, in the name of Jesus.

30. No rod or no buckle will be put in my nostrils, in the name of Jesus.

31. Sounds of boiling pots and burning boilers manifesting in my nostrils, be neutralized, in the name of Jesus.

32. The breath of the Lord will remain in my nostrils, in the name of Jesus.

33. I turn off the fire of the kingdom of darkness burning in my nostrils, in the name of Jesus.

34. I stir out of my nose the ring of the spirit husband / spirit wife, in the name of Jesus.

35. My nostrils, be cured of evil defects, in the name of Jesus.

36. Lord, revive my sense of smell, in the name of Jesus.

37. Gold ring on my nose stripping me of my faculties, fall and be broken, in the name of Jesus.

38. Astral hand squeezing my nose, be put into pieces, in the name of Jesus.

39. On this day, Lord, remove from my nose the branches of the spiritual world, in the name of Jesus.

40. I put to flight the powers that make my nose a control tower, in the name of Jesus.
41. I reject the breath of death introduced into my nostrils, in the name of Jesus.
42. I declare that the breath of life in my nostrils will not be converted to that of death, in the name of Jesus.
43. Any power that would like to evacuate what I ate through my nostrils, renounce your evil plans, in the name of Jesus.
44. Foods or beverages entered through the door of my mouth will not come out through my nostrils, in the name of Jesus.
45. I plead the blood of Jesus on the nostrils of the forces of darkness, in the name of Jesus.
46. Let the smoke coming out the nostrils of the forces of darkness destroy them, in the name of Jesus.

CHAPTER X

THE FORCES THAT DESTROY MARRIAGES (PART 1)

In the two following chapters, we will address the forces that destroy marriages. Just before, let's take a look at the first marriage of God's creation.

10.1. FIRST MARRIAGE OF CREATION

In the beginning, Adam lived in the Garden of Eden. After giving a name to each of the animals, he found no help meet for him. His desire to be with a woman caught the attention of the Lord. God allowed man the choice to express his desire to have a companion and then gave him one. Since Creation, man gave up loneliness. His appetite for a companion prompted the Almighty to create Eve. The Lord brought her to Adam, and he took her as his wife (Genesis 2:20-23). Beloved, the Creator established marriage in the Garden of Eden. Jehovah and the angels witnessed the marriage of Adam and Eve. From that moment, the first couple had a very good married life until the serpent visited them.

Following their dialogue with the serpent, Adam and Eve sinned against their Creator. So God gave them laws they should respect for the smooth running of their home. Then he chased out man from the Garden of Eden (Genesis 3:23). Note that before the Fall of Man, some rules on marriage already existed (Genesis 2:18 and 24). Now that he was expelled from paradise, the first couple was experiencing this marriage differently. Sin ushered death in the first marriage. Unfortunately, the marriage of Eden was lost. God gave it once, and human beings did not manage it well. In these times, marriage between man and woman is the one based on the laws given to the first couple after the Fall and other biblical principles presented thereafter.

No text in the scriptures informs us that Adam and Eve quarreled, brawled, separated, or were unfaithful to each other. If the marital life of the first couple was tumultuous, the Bible would have warned us. The couple lived a peaceful marriage because they respected the principles laid down in the book of the law. The following table summarizes the biblical principles for married men and women.

Table 8:   Summary of biblical principles for married men and women

		Men	Women
Old Testament	*Before the Fall*	The Creator has testified that a man should leave his parents and cleave to his wife (Genesis 2:24).	The woman was placed beside the man as a help meet (Genesis 2:18).
	After the Fall	The Lord said that man will rule over his wife (Genesis 3:16). God told the man he would eat by the sweat of his brow. Man had to work to feed his family (Genesis 3:19).	God told the woman that her desire shall be to her husband (Genesis 3:16).
New Testament		God has placed the husband as the head of the wife (1 Corinthians 11:3). God commanded man to love his wife (Ephesians 5:25).	The woman must cover her head to wear the symbol of the authority of her husband (1 Corinthians 11:10, NKJV). The woman was instructed to submit to her husband as unto the Lord (Ephesians 5:22).

Beloved, the enemy of your marriage is not your wife or your husband but the old serpent. If he was able to infiltrate in Eden to lead Adam and Eve to sin against the Lord, this evil spirit will do the same against your marriage. In trickery, the serpent easily polluted Adam's marriage in the Garden of Eden. Adam and Eve lost the privilege they enjoyed in their marriage. As a result of their sin, the Almighty established laws for their marriage and then expelled them out of Eden. These laws enabled Adam and Eve to know their position and role in their home. Despite the fact that they were expelled from the Garden of Eden, the dissatisfied serpent followed them with the intention of harming their homes. This cherub precipitated out of the heavens holds weapons he uses to destroy marriages. At present, let us look at some of these weapons described in the Bible: *adultery*, children conceived out of wedlock, the strange gods and the spirits of Mammon.

10.2. ADULTERY

In this section, we will cover the adulterous woman and Potiphar's wife.

10.2.1. The adulterous woman

Adultery is a weapon used by the devil to destroy marriages. It is defined as follows:

> Voluntary sexual intercourse between a married man and someone other than his wife or between a married woman and someone other than her husband. (*Merriam-Webster Online*, 2013)

Once a person has within him a spirit of adultery, this person will be unfaithful. Let us read the story of the adulterous woman in the book of Proverbs:

> Come, let us take our fill of love until morning; Let us delight ourselves with love. For my husband is not at home; He has gone on a long journey; He has taken a bag of money with him, and will come home

on the appointed day." With her enticing speech
she caused him to yield, with her flattering lips she
seduced him. Immediately he went after her, as an ox
goes to the slaughter, Or as a fool to the correction
of the stocks, till an arrow struck his liver. As a bird
hastens to the snare, He did not know it would cost
his life. Now therefore, listen to me, my children;
Pay attention to the words of my mouth: Do not let
your heart turn aside to her ways. Do not stray into
her paths; For she has cast down many wounded,
And all who were slain by her were strong men. Her
house is the way to hell, descending to the chambers
of death. (Proverbs 7:18-27, NKJV)

Here are the lessons learned from this text. First of all, a couple
who spends the whole night making love (Proverbs 7:18) needs
to be delivered from this anomaly. Then while this couple was
together in their house, the spirits of adultery did not manifest
in this woman. Everything was for the best, and peace reigned in
the home. From the time the husband went on a business trip,
the spirits of adultery rose up against this woman and pushed
her to be unfaithful to her husband. Some wives do not know
how to control themselves when their husband is away. During
the absence of their husbands, these women bring in men and
defile their marital bed. These women, blinded by the spirit of
adultery, are not shy about the fact that there may be children
or neighbors around them. They are stubborn at the cost of
their marriage and to the shame of their family. When men see
such scenes affect the marriage of their friend or neighbor, they
wonder how those women dared to take a lover in the marital
bed. Aren't there hotels where they can go? Since the Word of
God deals with this class of situation, normally such acts will
happen again till today.

Furthermore, it is possible that a man can be adulterous. Many people, who have committed adultery have seen the destruction of their homes and their reputation. The spirits of adultery publicly humiliated some very beloved public figures. The forty-second president of the United States, Bill Clinton, and the basketball star Kobe Bryant and the well-known golfer Tiger Woods are just a few examples. In addition, through their songs, artists encourage more people to the sin of adultery. I quote an artist from Cameroon named Sergeo Polo who had a hit song "The Husband of Another Is Sweet." I bet all those who dance the music of these singers end up later in the trap of the spirit of adultery. Yet the Word of God says,

> Whoever commits adultery with a woman lacks understanding; He who does so destroys his own soul. (Proverbs 6:32, NKJV)

Eating the fruit of adultery will only lead to distress in the lives of those who practice this activity.

10.2.2. Attraction to a servant

In this section, we will discuss Abram and Potiphar's wife.

Sarai, Abram's wife, suggested that he go to her Egyptian servant Hagar to have a child (Genesis 16:1-3). Abram could have refused this suggestion. Indeed, God had already promised to give him an offspring (Genesis 15:4-5). The proposal of Abram's wife can be compared to the fruit that Eve gave Adam. Abram was a wealthy and powerful man. He enjoyed the respect of kings. Despite his high reputation and his indefinite number of wealth, the spirits of adultery eventually brought him toward the servant of his wife. So far, the act that happened in the home of

Sarai continues to take place. Women find their husbands in bed with their handmaid, their cook, or the caretaker of their child.

The same situation seems equally possible in a wife, as we shall see for Potiphar's wife in the following story. Joseph ended up in Egypt as a slave at the age of seventeen. Potiphar, an influential man in the government of Pharaoh, took Joseph as a servant in his house. Potiphar's wife, who had in her the spirit of adultery, turned her eyes on the young servant of her husband. One morning, after Potiphar was away at work, his wife offered Joseph to sleep with her in the marital home (Genesis 39:7-12).

We can assume that Potiphar was already beyond his forties and his wife also. Joseph was an errand boy, while Potiphar was a military leader, a respected man in the nation. How come his wife had been able to demean herself at this level? Why go to a servant who could not be compared to her husband?

What do we notice in this condition? First, the spirits of adultery had pushed this woman toward Joseph. However, he was younger, and he could even be her son. In addition, the woman went to a man who did not have the social status of her husband. Similarly, the spirit of adultery headed her toward someone she hired in her house. What Joseph lived in the house of Potiphar continues to occur until now. The spirit of adultery leads married women to cheat on their husbands with people who are employed by their spouses. This spirit brings women to be attracted to young men. When some men go to work, these strange men will go after them to have a nice time with their wives in their homes. This phenomenon is very prominent in today's society. Having said that, married women should pray against this spirit before the devil uses it to humiliate and destroy their homes. What a shame for family members to hear that their sister was sent away by her husband for committing adultery with a man her husband employs! Who will have the courage to advocate for their sister to this man?

10.3. THE CHILDREN CONCEIVED OUT OF WEDLOCK

In Matthew 1:18 and 19, the Bible reports that Mary was engaged to Joseph. The latter was found pregnant by the virtue of the Holy Spirit before they lived together. Therefore, Mary was pregnant when she got married. She hid her situation from Joseph. The child she was carrying was from the Spirit of God and not her spouse. Later, Joseph was informed of this pregnancy, and there was torment in their homes.

Thus, some women were already pregnant by another man before marriage, but they had concealed it from their fiancé. Yet other women conceive children with a different man than their husband and pretend that the pregnancy belongs to him. It is common for men to take care of children in their house that come from another biological parent.

My sisters, how will you react the day your husband will know that one of the children comes from the seed of another man? My brothers, will you have the heart of Joseph not to be willing to make your wife a public example? Once you discover that one of the children in your home belongs to someone else, what will you do? Will you be able to keep quiet to save your marriage? Joseph's example should teach all of us. God finally took action in his household, and peace was restored. Similarly, the man of Galilee will intervene in your marriage, whatever trials you are going through. In case you and your sweetheart are secretly separated, the right hand of the Lord is powerful enough to bring you back to one another.

10.4. THE STRANGE GODS (GENESIS 31:33-35)

When Jacob left the house of his father-in-law, Laban, with his wives and children, he briefly settled at mount Gilead. In this place, he put up tents for all his clan. Pursued by his father-in-law, Laban, the latter found him camping in the mountains. Laban accused Jacob of having brought with him his strange gods.

> Now Rachel had taken the household idols, put them in the camel's saddle, and sat on them. And Laban searched all about the tent but did not find them. And she said to her father, "Let it not displease my lord that I cannot rise before you, for the manner of women is with me." And he searched but did not find the household idols. (Genesis 31:34-35, NKJV)

When Rachel left her father's house with her husband, Jacob, for their new location, she brought the household idols that belonged to Laban. These gods of her father had already helped her to fight divinely against her sister, as mentioned in a French version of the Bible (Genesis 30:8, LSG). She finally had a son whom she named Joseph. Unfortunately, the home of this mother had tribulations. To maintain her place in her marriage as a second wife, Rachel sat on the fetishes she had brought from her father's house. Using these fetishes, she could hold Jacob's heart to be closer to him than his other wives.

At the present day, wives act as Rachel in their homes, to the point of afflicting their husbands. Thus, spouses are subjected by the flesh of their flesh while ignoring that these use evil powers to dominate, control, or manipulate them. These partners believe the love they feel toward their spouses is real. They are unaware that their wives are using the powers of darkness to turn their heart to them. Some men and women receive fetishes from the hands of their parents when they were about to marry, to assure or protect their marriage so it will not collapse.

Moreover, Laban searched the house of Jacob to get his gods. My brothers, maybe you need to put your house upside down to find out if your wife hides fetishes that she uses against you. Sisters, do as much to reassure yourself that your husband has not placed strange gods in a corner of the house.

Additionally, the fact that Rachel was sitting on household idols indicates that many married women have inherited witchcraft from their families. These women left their family home to their household already being witches; however, their husbands do not know. The home of Jacob was confronted with the presence of two types of gods: the one worshiped by Jacob and that served by Rachel. The youngest daughter of Laban was opposed to her husband, according to their spiritual difference (Genesis 2:18). Not knowing the truth, this dissimilarity brought Jacob to curse his wife. This is how, later, Rachel found death, giving birth to Benjamin. Here are the negative consequences suffered by homes when strange gods are served by one of the partners. The end proves to be tragic for that home.

10.5. THE SPIRIT OF MAMMON (PROVERBS 7:20)

The spirits of Mammon also belong to the category of forces used by Satan to disrupt families. Some households would be at peace if there was transparency in the management of finances. In some couples, this has created a lack of confidence to the point where everyone has to manage their resources without having the other party interfering. In these homes, the husband does not put an eye on what makes his wife, and vice versa. Everyone cares about his personal expenses. Dear brothers and sisters, God said in Genesis, "And they shall be one flesh" (Genesis 2:24c). This statement means that once married, you become one. What comes from the woman belongs to the man as what is to the man belongs to the woman. Beloved, if your earnings are yours alone and in the event you keep your possessions only for you, know that, right now, your relationship is composed of two entities, not one. This type of attitude gives rise to problems.

In Proverbs 7:20, the woman said that her husband left with the bag of money on a long journey. This lady knew when her husband would return. However, she did not know exactly where he was going. So do some men in their homes. Once a dispute arises with their wives, they rush to the bank, empty the accounts, and retreat to an unknown destination. Thinking they hurt their wives, they are harming themselves. It is quite possible that this money is the result of the work of this woman. I imagine that there was a power struggle in the home before the man left with the money. Maybe this man used his wife as an automatic teller machine (ATM). She worked hard, and whenever money came in, he went to waste it. Some men are married to women only for their fortune.

My brothers, should you do business outside your home with sums earned by the sweat of the brow of your wife or that you use your wealth without informing your wife, you will now be acting wrongly. Now husbands and wives discuss the financial situation of your household by developing the management plan for your income. Each spouse is invited to talk openly to each other. The couple must have and bring their spending plans by checking all the inputs and outputs of money.

In the same vein, wives should be careful to avoid the misfortune that came to the wife of the sons of the prophets in 2 Kings 4:1. This man had probably concealed the state of his finances to his wife. What was the surprise of the latter the day the creditor appeared at her door to claim her two children in order to repay the debt of her husband! People lose their properties because their husbands or wives have contracted debts by pledging their assets without slipping a word. The spouses will be surprised on the day that justice seizes their wealth gained with so much effort.

Finally, in an indebted household, the couple should be looking for solutions. Beloved, invoke the Lord so that he will come to your help. The God of miracles has not changed. As he fed four thousand people with five loaves of bread and two fishes, he will work for you. Do not let debt kill your marriage or bring you to the grave as what happened to the son of the prophets. The section of prayers below will help you get up against the forces that are obstinate to ruin your marriage. God delivers such powers into your hands. Treat them harshly for them to be removed from your marriage.

10.6. Prayer section

1. I strike off delusion, the enemy of my marriage, in the name of Jesus.
2. I transform into madness the cunning of the serpent affecting my marriage, in the name of Jesus.
3. I crush the head of the serpent located in the body of my husband / my wife, in the name of Jesus.
4. I stone to death the forces using my husband / my wife to destroy me, in the name of Jesus.

5. Any object given to my husband / my wife by an impostor and used to bewitch me, I destroy their effects, in the name of Jesus.

6. By the waters of Noah, I destroy the forces that divert the desires of my husband / my wife, in the name of Jesus.

7. I bring judgments on the spirits of domination, control, and manipulation living in the body of my husband / my wife, in the name of Jesus.

8. By the blood of Jesus, I abolish traditional laws governing my marriage, in the name of Jesus.

9. *For men:* Any power in the world of darkness preventing my wife to be submissive to me, be disgraced, in the name of Jesus.

10. *For men:* Any power preventing me to love my wife, be stoned, in the name of Jesus.

11. *For women:* Any power in the world of darkness preventing my husband to be the head of our home, be disgraced, in the name of Jesus.

12. *For women:* Any power preventing me to love my husband, be stoned, in the name of Jesus.

13. I bind and chase the spirits of adultery making me defile the matrimony bed, in the name of Jesus.

14. *For men:* Lord, punish the spirits of adultery giving my wife the desire to sleep with the men I employ, in the name of Jesus.

15. *For women:* Lord, punish the spirits of adultery giving my husband the desire to sleep with the women I employ, in the name of Jesus.

16. Lord, judge the adulterous spirits in the lives of men/ women who covet my wife / my husband, in the name of Jesus.

17. I chain the spirit of adultery and murder in the lives of people obstinate to defile my bed, in the name of Jesus.

18. *For men:* Lord, expel from my wife the spirits drawing her toward young men, in the name of Jesus.

19. *For women:* Lord, expel from my husband the spirits drawing him toward young women, in the name of Jesus.

20. *For men:* Lord, make my wife a virtuous woman, in the name of Jesus.

21. *For women:* Lord, make my husband a good man, in the name of Jesus.

22. I break the neck of the forces using my tongue to slander my husband / my wife, in the name of Jesus.

23. On this day, I put an end to all secret splits between me and my husband / my wife, in the name of Jesus.

24. Angel of the Lord, appear in the dream of my husband / my wife, and give him/her the necessary solution to our marriage, in the name of Jesus.

25. Any problem that has followed my husband / my wife from his/her father's house to our matrimonial home, lose your control, in the name of Jesus.

26. Power of the foundation of my husband / my wife, who wrapped him/her during the engagement, be torn, in the name of Jesus.

27. By the blood of Jesus, I neutralize the accusations made against me by my in-laws, in the name of Jesus.

28. Spirit of witchcraft consulted by my in-laws, harassing me day and night, be roasted by fire, in the name of Jesus.

29. By the divine fire, I burn the foreign gods, fetishes, or evil objects introduced in this house by my husband / my wife, in the name of Jesus.

30. Divine fire, burn the fetish on which my husband / my wife is sitting on, in the name of Jesus.

31. Divine fire, consume the evil powers used by my husband / my wife to fight me, in the name of Jesus.

32. I break the curses pronounced on my life by my husband / my wife, in the name of Jesus.

33. Any strange god worshiped by my husband / my wife in our home, be thrown into the lions' den, in the name of Jesus.

34. Lord, deliver my marriage from the spirits of Mammon, in the name of Jesus.

35. Any force that causes my husband / my wife to waste money unnecessarily, go in the valley of the shadow of death, in the name of Jesus.

36. Every spirit in the spiritual world talking to my husband / my wife, be thrown into the fire, in the name of Jesus.

37. Every spirit of witchcraft that inhabit my in-laws and is pursuing me, be buried by the grave digger, in the name of Jesus.

38. Any spirit of debt that wants to bring my husband / my wife to the grave, release him and let him go, in the name of Jesus.

39. I disgrace any power that wants my children, my belongings, and my properties to be taken away because of the debt contracted by my husband / my wife, in the name of Jesus.

40. O Lord, deliver my marriage and my family from the spirit of debt, in the name of Jesus.

41. Miraculous power of God that saved the sons of the widow from the hand of the creditor, set us free, in the name of Jesus.

42. Any spirit of debt that wants my husband / my wife to die and make me suffer in this land of the living, fall and rise no more, in the name of Jesus.

43. I shut the door of my house to any strange man / strange woman coming to my home to play with my wife / my husband when I'm not around, in the name of Jesus.

CHAPTER XI

THE FORCES THAT DESTROY MARRIAGES (PART 2)

Teachings about the forces that destroy marriages are presented as alarm bells from the Lord to help us improve the relationships in our homes and to fight the enemy who opposes peace in our marriage.

11.1. THE DISSIMILARITY

God is the founder of marriage, which is why he says in his Word,

> And the Lord God said, It is not good that the man should be alone; I will make him an help meet for him. (Genesis 2:18)

Beloved, it is possible that you and your partner are not alike. You should make an effort now to become so. Otherwise, your dissimilarity will open a door to the enemy. Households where couples are contrary seem to be a territory conquered by the serpent. Being similar to each other does not mean that both husband and wife must be involved in the same career, go to the same church, or take part in the same activities. What God alluded in Genesis 2:18 is that the spirit that is inside a husband should be the same as that inside his wife.

When a woman has within her the spirit of Jesus Christ and her companion has the same spirit, these two people are alike. It may be that one of the parties in a couple have the spirit of God, while the other does not, as was the case of Jacob and Rachel. Despite the physical attraction that these two felt for each other, the spirit within each of them made them different beings. There was discord in their home. In Genesis 30:1, Rachel, daughter of Laban, threatens to commit suicide if Jacob refused to give her a child. At this point, she did not act like a help to her husband. In this type of situation, the unclean spirit within one of the party must be driven out so that the spirit of God takes place.

Beloved, may Jesus Christ be the cornerstone of your marriage, the rock on which all spouses must stand. Thus, the couple will regularly pray with each other and bring their differences before the Lord. The spouses will study together the Word of God and act according to what it says. A woman will be patient with her husband, while the latter will show her meekness and temperance.

In this chapter, we will see new elements that uses our adversary to create discord in the home. The book of the law is life for our souls and for all that concerns us. In his Word, the Lord promises to make our enemies our footstool on the sole condition that we remain at his right hand. In the next sections, we will discuss lack of affection, disobedience, family, marriage by abduction, and lack of attraction.

11.2. Lack of affection

A few years ago, a sister told me she had a lack of affection for her husband. She confided in me that she felt the urge to stab him every time he approached her. I advised her to go quickly for deliverance, which she did. I saw this woman again a few days later; she was completely changed. She told me after the meeting of deliverance prayer, she saw a bird come out of her house when she came home. Since that time, her affection for her husband was restored. The desire to stab the latter had disappeared.

> Without understanding, covenantbreakers, without natural affection, implacable, unmerciful. (Romans 1:31)

You know, the lack of affection expresses the condition in which a man or woman experiences a lack of interest in his or her spouse. The spiritual bond that linked these people, as described in Genesis 2:24, no longer exists. The devil has broken it. When the affection in a couple is missing, there will be a lack of love between spouses. The hearts of these people will be saddened. They will spend their time blaming each other. A man will take pleasure in criticizing his wife regularly and constantly arguing with her. For her part, the woman will have her eyes fixed on the shortcomings of her husband. In the end, one of the partners could be abandoned, neglected, or put away because of lack of affection. Also, according to this scripture, the affection between two people can be natural or demonic. Only the Word of God or his power can help us to discern the type of affection people have for one another.

In the following two sections, we will see how deeds and obscure words can be the cause of lack of affection.

11.3. THE DEEDS

> And to esteem them very highly in love for their
> work's sake. And be at peace among yourselves.
> (1 Thessalonians 5:13)

The works of spouses can bring them together or apart from one another. When a man ceases to take care of his wife and vice versa, this attitude can lead to a lack of affection or esteem in a home.

Beloved, your actions can change your marriage. The esteem of the spouses will depend on initiatives each is taking. A partner who spends less time with the bone of his bones, confides more to friends or family members, pays less attention to the other person, constantly forgets their words, considers less their opinions, or does not appreciate the little efforts that the other made will be deprived of affection from their sweetheart. Instead, in a couple where the spouses multiply the positive gestures toward each other, their commitment will be increased. Thus, peace will reign in their marriage.

11.4. OBSCURE WORDS

> May no one extend kindness to him or take pity on
> his fatherless children. (Psalm 109:12, NIV)

In this psalm, David, son of Jesse, implores the Lord to act against his adversary. The judgment that King David asks his Creator to bring against his opponent is that none extends *kindness* unto him. The word *kindness* means the following:

> 1) A kind deed: favor; 2) Archaic: affection. (*Merriam-Webster Online*, 2013)

The word *kind* signifies the following:

> 1) Affectionate, loving; 2) Of a sympathetic or helpful nature; 3) Of a forbearing nature: gentle. (*Merriam-Webster Online*, 2013)

In this passage, David wishes that his God encourages those around his enemy to hate him. God's mission was to prevent his or her spouse and children from loving him. The Lord was going to destroy the home of David's enemy, using the lack of affection or kindness as a weapon.

In a couple, the lack of affection can be caused by spiritual forces. When people want to ruin an individual, they pronounce obscure words against his union. These wicked people cry out to their deities or invoke them so that they damage the attachment a person has for his partner. This partner will unconsciously be under the influence of a demon, which will use this person to destroy his home.

In the book of Isaiah 54:7, the word declares,

> For a small moment have I forsaken thee; but with great mercies will I gather thee.

The French version (LSG) of this verse states,

> Quelques instants je t'avais abandonnée, Mais avec une grande affection je t'accueillerai.

God proclaims the restoration of homes that were destroyed by the lack of affection. These homes will be restored by the power of God. The husband who left his wife for a while will come back to her with great affection, and vice versa. The Lord will introduce in each one the desire to welcome another.

Dear sister, dear brother, with God, all things are possible. As soon as you notice a lack of *attraction* between you and your partner, seek God immediately. He will send a great affection in your home to restore peace.

11.5. THE DISOBEDIENCE

> But the queen Vashti refused to come at the king's commandment by his chamberlains: therefore was the king very wroth, and his anger burned in him. (Esther 1:12)

At first glance, disobedience is a force used by the devil to break up marriages. When a wife disobeys her husband, she jeopardizes her marriage. This is what happened to Queen Vashti. King Ahasuerus held a feast for his princes and his servants. He sent the seven chamberlains that served in his presence to bring Vashti, the queen, so that she could be presented to the people and to the great ones. Vashti refused to come, and her behavior heightened the king's anger. After consulting the elders to know what sentence to take following the conduct of the queen, King Ahasuerus dismissed his wife to marry another one (Esther 1:19).

Why was the resolution of the king so severe?

First, we notice that King Ahasuerus decided to send away his wife under the influence of anger. Indeed, he felt publicly humiliated by her. He was still furious at the time the decision was made. Later, when he had softened, his thoughts turned toward the one his heart had loved. The king regretted having repudiated his wife in haste (Esther 2:1).

Secondly, the king's wise men encouraged him to get rid of Queen Vashti despite the fact that he had the choice to dismiss her or not. People who act in anger and follow bad advice most often end up regretting their actions. However, beloved, in the case of your marriage, the best way to proceed is to consult the Lord after your irritation is gone.

Thirdly, the act of the queen toward her husband was disappointing. However, before judging the behavior of the queen, in what state was the king when he called to his wife?

> On the seventh day, when the heart of the king was merry with wine [. . .]. (Esther 1:10a)

When the monarch ordered his eunuchs to bring Queen Vashti before him to show her *beauty* to the people, his heart was delighted by wine. His *majesty* was drunk. It is in this state of drunkenness that he wanted to present the queen to the officials, which displeased her. The king's drunkenness pushed Vashti to disobey him. When the sire made up his mind, he had forgotten that he was under the influence of strong wine. He could only see that his wife had dishonored him before his guests without trying to understand the cause of her disobedience.

We understand that men who devote themselves to alcohol go through similar situations in their homes. While they complain about the behavior of their wives, they refuse to give up strong liquors. It is when they are inebriated that they want to talk or have a causerie with their wives. Woe to them if they disappoint their husbands who are drunk.

Unfortunately, strong wine contributed to the downfall of many marriages. Also, some women have lost patience with their husbands in this case. Suppose that Queen Vashti had simply obeyed her husband, despite his drunkenness; the king would have stayed married to her. My sister, disobedience is as reprehensible as the sin of witchcraft (1 Samuel 15:23). To the best of your ability, obey your husband even though he would have provoked you. Then once he is sober, you can address him with love on his bad behavior. The affection of a man toward his sweetheart will be doubled if she acts so (2 Corinthians 7:15).

11.6. FAMILY

The family is another force used by the enemy to destroy marriages. Let us read the story of Samson the judge during his wedding:

> So his father went down unto the woman: and Samson made there a feast; for so used the young men to do. And it came to pass, when they saw him, that they brought thirty companions to be with him. And Samson said unto them, I will now put forth a riddle unto you: if ye can certainly declare it me within the seven days of the feast, and find it out, then I will give you thirty sheets and thirty change of garments. (Judges 14:10-12)

Samson and his parents went down to Timnath, a city where the woman he fell in love with dwelt. Upon arrival, this judge made a feast for seven days, as was the custom among the people. The parents-in-law of Samson invited their family to attend the wedding of their daughter. During the wedding ceremonies, the brothers-in-law of Samson came to keep him company. The groom proposed a riddle to them. The playing conditions were the following: Samson would hand over to his brothers-in-law thirty sheets and thirty change of garments if they were answer to the riddle. In the contrary, it would be Samson's brothers-in-law that would have to give him thirty sheets and thirty change of garments (Judges 14:13).

Still in the book of Judges 14, in verse 15, the brothers of Samson's wife came to ask her to persuade her husband to explain to them the enigma; otherwise, they would burn her as well as the house of her father. In verses 16 and 17, the Bible describes the details of what this woman did to have this information. Once notified by her husband on the riddle, she disclosed the secret to the children of her people. This betrayal led to the anger of Samson. The situation went from bad to worse. Samson gave to his brothers-in-law the thirty sheets and thirty change of garments he obtained by killing thirty men and stripping them afterward. He returned furious in his parents' house, without his wife. Later, she was given to his companion whom he had used as his friend (verses 19 and 20).

Here are the lessons to be learned from what happened to Samson and his wife. Samson's wife was more attached to the children of her people than to her husband. In fact, she listened to the voices of family members more than Samson. In addition, she gave them the secret of Samson instead of defending and keeping his riddle confidential. The people of Timnath used Samson's wife for their advantage. Her brothers were more concerned with the clothes that Samson would bring them than the well-being of their sister. Unwisely, the wife of Samson tormented and threatened him for the benefit of her family. She hid from her husband the threats of her people, an attitude that endangered her life and that of her parents. Finally, she bowed to the demands of her parents by going with the friend of her husband without thinking of the consequences of her act.

Alas, the end of their marriage was tragic. Samson destroyed the plantations of the Philistines. To get revenge, the people of Timnath burned Samson's wife and his father-in-law (Judges 15:5-6). The words spoken by the sons of Timnites was accomplished against the wife of Samson (Judges 14:15).

Beloved, your marriage can be a stumbling block for you and your father's house. Spare your parents about what is going on in your home. Your life as a couple is not an open book. For example, does your family need to be informed of the incontinence of your partner?

To return to the story of Samson, his wife was endowed twice. First by Samson, then by his friend, who ended up going to her. It is flippantly that his parents kept the dowry they had taken from the hands of their first son-in-law. They offered their son-in-law to give him, in exchange, the younger sister of his wife (Judges 15:2).

My sisters, if you let your parents take several dowries on you, for different men, you may end up like the wife of Samson. This lady has never enjoyed her first or her second marriage. Why allow your parents to destroy your marriage because of greed? My brothers, you married a woman who had already been given to another man without restoring the dowry? You'd better remedy this situation that can become a stumbling block in your home. My dear sister, have you gotten married to a man who was supposed to get married with your senior sister but gave up at the last moment to choose you instead of her? Have you been married to a man by an arrangement made between him and your parents without your agreement? No matter what the reason could be, you need to pray so the devil will not use that doorway to destroy your marriage.

11.7. MARRIAGE BY ABDUCTION

A sister, for whom I prayed, explained to me how a curse was placed on her family lineage by her great-grandparents. She told me that her grandmother got married without having her grandfather meeting the parents of his future wife, which means her grandma. As soon as the parents of her grandmother learned that their daughter had married without consulting them, they pronounced curses on their new son-in-law.

Now, let us read the Word of God in the book of Judges in chapter 21:

> Therefore they commanded the children of Benjamin, saying, Go and lie in wait in the vineyards; And see, and, behold, if the daughters of Shiloh come out to dance in dances, then come ye out of the vineyards, and catch you every man his wife of the daughters of Shiloh, and go to the land of Benjamin. And it shall be, when their fathers or their brethren come unto us to complain, that we will say unto them, Be favourable unto them for our sakes: because we reserved not to each man his wife in the war: for ye did not give unto them at this time, that ye should be guilty. (Judges 21:20-22)

Previously, an act of violence had been performed on the wife of a Levite in Gibeah of Benjamin. Following this action, there was a conflict between the tribes of Israel and the tribe of Benjamin (Judges 20:4-14). The Benjaminites refused to give away the perverts responsible of the wicked action so that the evil would be removed in Israel. Instead, they opted to go to war but lost the battle. At the end of hostilities, the people of Israel disdained to give their daughters in marriage unto a Benjaminite. Later, the Israelites felt remorse about the tribe of Benjamin, their brother. To prevent that this tribe be cut off from Israel, the elders of Israel decided to provide women to the Benjaminites who had survived the battle.

Thereafter, the elders of Israel gave to the Benjaminites orders to lie in ambush in the vineyards and to take one woman for wife. When the daughters of Shiloh would come out to dance, each Benjaminite would emerge from the vineyards and take one of the daughters of Shiloh for her to become his wife. Then they returned to their country.

The Benjaminites looked carefully before removing those they had chosen. Moreover, the daughters of Shiloh, who went out dancing, were unaware that they were given in marriage by the elders. They had decided the fate of the girls without their opinion or that of their parents. Men were placed in ambush to bring them in their country without the girls saying good-bye to their families. These ladies had to go through marriage without the assurance of seeing their families again one day. The parents of these girls learned from other sources what had been decided by the elders. Any chance to see their daughters or meet their sons-in-law was lost. Complaints or claims of the relatives of these young women against the men of Benjamin were useless. Indeed, the elders took upon themselves the responsibility of this decision.

On that day, these young ladies left their family home for the last time. They left the house of their father for their matrimonial home by a plot, without shouts of joy, dances, and tambourines. Yet the men of Benjamin, happy to get the women, were acting on the orders of the ancients. The Benjaminites were sinless. The abduction was the mode of marriage granted to them.

Finally, marriage by abduction is rooted in this story. Some people still behave the way Benjaminites acted towards the daughters of Shiloh. They do so, not because it is an order that was given to them, but because Satan is behind their actions. They are placed in churches, schools, universities, business, clubs, workplace, public places, etc., in order to catch subtlety a naïve woman to marry, without following a normal procedure. A marriage is consummated under the basis of abduction, when a man marries a woman without consulting her parents, either before or after marriage. This couple will open a doorway through which the devil will come to destroy their homes. This individual will be considered a thief. The parents of the wife will be very unhappy with their son-in-law. Nevertheless, the people who got married in this way will have to go back to their family-in-law and give them the dowry. Thus, they avoid a curse that will affect their children later.

Like what happened to the daughters of Shiloh, some women came out of their parents' homes one day and never returned or were no longer seen by their families. They married without informing their parents and did not go back to present their husbands to their families.

My sister, what happened to the girls of Shiloh may be similar to your situation. Still, better late than never, as the saying goes. May your husband and you go back to see your parents to solve this wrong. The grace of God will go with you.

11.8. THE LACK OF ATTRACTION

By definition, *attraction*

> is a force acting mutually between particles of matter,
> tending to draw them together, and resisting their
> separation. (*Merriam-Webster Online*, 2013)

It can happen that a woman would lack attachment toward her husband. The opposite also exists. A person may feel disgust for the body of his partner. Many reasons can be given by each to defend their position. Each year, the cosmetics industry raises millions of dollars through the public using multiple *beauty* products to change their appearance under pretense of taking care of their physical body. In addition, some partners do not care for their appearance when they know they are a couple.

Now let us read this verse from the book of Isaiah:

> He grew up before him like a tender shoot, and like a
> root out of dry ground. He had no beauty or majesty
> to attract us to him, nothing in his appearance that
> we should desire him. (Isaiah 53:2, NIV)

This verse is a prophecy referring to our Lord and Savior, Jesus Christ. It speaks about what he will go through—the affliction, oppression, and grief he must endure for us to be saved. However, by going through this hardship or trouble, he was rejected. In this verse, two words are mentioned to describe what may attract a couple one to another: *beauty* and *majesty.* *Beauty* refers to the physical part, while *majesty* refers to the spiritual part.

Now let us consider each of these words, starting with beauty.

> He hath no beauty. (Isaiah 53:2b)

Beauty means the following:

> 1) The quality or aggregate of qualities in a person or thing that gives pleasure to the senses or pleasurably exalts the mind or spirit: loveliness; 2) A beautiful person or thing; especially: a beautiful woman. (*Merriam-Webster Online*, 2013)

When a woman is beautiful, she will attract her husband toward her, and vice versa. The desire to seduce the loved one or look pretty can motivate men or women to take care of their body through exercise and adorning themselves with jewelry, perfume, cologne, or weaves. But in fact, what does your partner look like without artifice, makeup, perfume, jewelry, or designer clothes? In Psalm 139:14, David said to the Lord,

> I will praise thee; for I am fearfully and wonderfully made: marvellous are thy works; and that my soul knoweth right well.

Beloved, you are a marvelous work of the Lord and a wonderful creature. The situation you are going through may be what makes your husband or wife not find you attractive. Indeed, trials in one's life can make him unattractive. Then his beauty will not be seen. When people look at such a person, they will only see his affliction. His problem has covered his beauty. Once he gets out from that situation, his appearance will change.

> Or majesty. (Isaiah 53:2b)

The word *majesty* is defined as follows:

> 1) Sovereign power, authority, or dignity; 2) Greatness or splendor of quality or character. (*Merriam-Webster Online*, 2013)

Let us read what the psalmist declares in Psalm 21:5 (NIV),

> Through the victories you gave, his glory is great;
> you have bestowed on him splendor and majesty.

The majesty is the power or authority that the Lord puts in his disciples to rule, be famous or popular, which will attract attention to the person. Satan also offers this type of majesty to his agent to be attractive, but it's different. When an individual moves away from Jesus, he will no longer radiate. Then the eyes of one's spouse will be turned away from him. This lack of power or authority will create trouble in his marriage.

Beloved, if your partner is no longer attracted to you despite all the efforts that you have provided to captivate their gaze, it is not over yet. You might not be beautiful in the sight of your partner, but you are still attractive by having in you majesty; this can only come from God. It is time for you to come closer to God and serve him with all your strength. Beloved, if God is with you, who can be against you?

11.9. CURSE

A curse is one of the ways through which the adversary uses to destroy marriages. Let us read some of what the Word says in the book of Amos:

Then Amaziah the priest of Bethel sent to Jeroboam king of Israel, saying, Amos hath conspired against thee in the midst of the house of Israel: the land is not able to bear all his words. For thus Amos saith, Jeroboam shall die by the sword, and Israel shall surely be led away captive out of their own land. (Amos 7:10-11)

During the time of King Jeroboam, Israel had turned away from the Lord to serve strange gods. What these priests were doing was wrong in the sight of the Lord. This is the reason why God sent prophet Amos, a man of God, to speak to them in his name. The criticisms of Amos displeased Amaziah, the priest of Bethel. This priest went to accuse the man of God before the king Jeroboam. Amaziah wanted, at all costs, to prevent Amos to prophesy in the name of the Lord. So he asked him to go into the land of Judah to do his prophecies.

Now let us read the answer of the prophet Amos to Amaziah, priest of Bethel:

Therefore thus saith the Lord; Thy wife shall be an harlot in the city, and thy sons and thy daughters shall fall by the sword, and thy land shall be divided by line; and thou shalt die in a polluted land: and Israel shall surely go into captivity forth of his land. (Amos 7:17)

The response of the prophet Amos at the priest of Bethel, following his threats, was the judgment that the Lord rendered against the priest, his family, and Israel. Through the mouth of his servant, God pronounced a sentence against the marriage of the priest of Bethel, stating that his wife had to disgrace herself in the city. To destroy the marriage of this priest, God chose to transform his wife into a *harlot* in the city where he lived.

A *harlot* is defined as a "prostitute" (*Merriam-Webster Online*, 2013).

A *prostitute* is defined as follows:

> 1) A woman who engages in promiscuous sexual intercourse especially for money: whore; 2) A male who engages in sexual and especially homosexual practices for money. (*Merriam-Webster Online*, 2013)

To return to our story, as soon as the word was spoken, the wife of Amaziah wandered in the town of Bethel, giving her body to immorality. The latter did not understand that her husband was the origin of this prostitution. I believe that this priest, wounded in his pride, found it difficult to know that his wife was sleeping elsewhere. All his efforts to stop his wife were useless because it was the hand of God himself who turned against his marriage.

Just like the priest, here's what couples experience in their homes. Some men repudiate their wives because of their unfaithfulness. Whatever means they have tried to stop the latter have not worked. These men do not know that they are the cause of this situation. They forget that a curse has been cast upon their wives due to their behavior. Ladies, if your husband runs after other women, divorce will not bring any solution. Find out if you are not the victim of a curse in response to your past actions. With respect to our churches, pastors' wives engage in sexual acts with members of the congregation; husbands are loving women in their community. However, no one discerns that a curse is the cause of their fall.

Beloved, the prayer below will enable the Lord to deliver your marriage from the evil one. I pray that his will be done in your home.

11.10. Prayer section

1. Lord, pour in my heart the love for my husband / my wife, in the name of Jesus.
2. Divine anger, scatter the spirits that move away from my heart the love I have for my husband / my wife, in the name of Jesus.
3. Lord, restore the foundation of my marriage, in the name of Jesus.
4. I render powerless the spirits sitting in the foundation of my marriage, in the name of Jesus.
5. Divine power, make my husband / my wife a help meet for me, in the name of Jesus.
6. Divine power, make me a help meet to my husband / my wife, in the name of Jesus.
7. Every spirit living inside my husband / my wife, different from the spirit of Christ in me, be expelled, in the name of Jesus.
8. Every spirit living inside my body, different from the spirit of Christ, existing in my husband / my wife, be dislodged, in the name of Jesus.
9. Destroy, O Lord, the forces that prevent peace to reign in my home, in the name of Jesus.
10. Any problem in my home prompting my husband / my wife to commit suicide, be humiliated and persecuted, in the name of Jesus.
11. I bind the spirits of suicide operating in the life of my husband / my wife, in the name of Jesus.

12. Any demon that prevents my husband / my wife to leave his/her father or mother and cleave to me, be powerless, in the name of Jesus.

13. King of kings, restore the attachment that was broken between my husband / my wife and me, in the name of Jesus.

14. Lord, ruin the affectionate kisses of those who covet my husband / my wife in their heart, in the name of Jesus.

15. My husband / my wife and I will be full of affection for each other, in the name of Jesus.

16. I bind and chase the spirits sent to keep my husband / my wife from maintaining affection for me, in the name of Jesus.

17. I cancel the obscure words devastating the affection between my husband / my wife and I, in the name of Jesus.

18. I cancel the enchantments pronounced against my marriage, in the name of Jesus.

19. I bind the spirits of disobedience hardening my husband / my wife, in the name of Jesus.

20. I confuse the language of the wise men of my village and of the spiritual world gathered to affect my marriage, in the name of Jesus.

21. Divine fire, consume the affection of the flesh in my marriage, in the name of Jesus.

22. *For men:* Voice of the Lord, break the affection of the spirit husband in the life of my wife, in the name of Jesus.

23. *For women:* Voice of the Lord, break the affection of the spirit wife in the life of my husband, in the name of Jesus.

24. Man of Galilee, multiply the affection between my husband / my wife and me, in the name of Jesus.

25. With great affection, I welcome my husband / my wife left or abandoned, in the name of Jesus.

26. Any foreign god invoked to break the affection between my husband / my wife and me, eat your own dung and drink your own piss, in the name of Jesus.

27. I trouble the words from the mouth confessing evil against my marriage, in the name of Jesus.

28. Every spirit in the water turning the affection of my husband / my wife away from me, be bitten by the divine serpent, in the name of Jesus.

29. The curses pronounced without cause on my marriage will have no effect on me, in the name of Jesus.

30. Lord, change the curse issued against me by my husband / my wife into blessing, in the name of Jesus.

31. *For men:* By the sword, I cut off the power of those who say that my wife will be a prostitute, in the name of Jesus.

32. *For women:* By the sword, I cut off the power of those who say that my husband will be a prostitute, in the name of Jesus.

33. Break, Lord, the curses issued against my husband / my wife because of my wrongdoing, in the name of Jesus.

34. Angels of the Lord, strike the spirits of prostitution ruining my marriage, in the name of Jesus.

35. Every demon in the private part of my husband / my wife come out and go in the dry places, in the name of Jesus.

36. This city will not be a stumbling block or an iron furnace for my marriage, in the name of Jesus.

37. I praise you, Lord, that my husband / my wife is wonderfully made, in the name of Jesus.

38. O Lord, place upon my husband / my wife splendor and majesty, in the name of Jesus.

39. Arise, Lord, and attract my husband / my wife toward me, in the name of Jesus.

40. My husband / my wife will extend his/her look toward me to support me because my heart is perfect toward him/her, in the name of Jesus.

41. O Lord, give me the qualities that will attract the eyes of my husband / my wife, in the name of Jesus.

42. I demolish the abominations that attract the eyes of my husband / my wife, in the name of Jesus.

43. Rebuke, Lord, the mouths who complain about my marriage, in the name of Jesus.

44. I demolished the foundation of marriage by abduction in my family, in the name of Jesus.

45. Divert, Lord, the feet of my husband / my wife on the road where are located women/men in ambush, in the name of Jesus.

46. Divine power, discourage men/women placed in ambush to take my wife / my husband, in the name of Jesus.

47. Any order issued by my ancestors concerning the marriages in my family, be blotted out by the bitter waters, in the name of Jesus.

48. My marriage will not be the way to hell, in the name of Jesus.

49. Any demon using me to torment my husband / my wife, perish by the sword, in the name of Jesus.

50. Defend, O Lord, the cause of my husband / my wife among my family, in the name of Jesus.

51. My mouth will not deliver my husband / my wife to those who seek his/her downfall, in the name of Jesus.

52. I separate myself from family members who want to use me to strip my husband / my wife, in the name of Jesus.

53. Chase, Lord, the princes who want to persuade me to reveal the secret of my husband / my wife, in the name of Jesus.

54. I cancel the dark words uttered during the ceremonies of my wedding, in the name of Jesus.

55. Any conflict between my husband / my wife and my family, receive an angelic intervention, in the name of Jesus.

56. The evil conceived against me by members of my family during my wedding ceremonies will produce nothingness, in the name of Jesus.

57. *For men:* O Lord, give me and my wife the capacity to return the dowry that her parents received for a wedding that she did not consume, in the name of Jesus.

58. *For women:* O Lord, give me and my husband the capability to restore the dowry that my parents received for a wedding that I did not consume, in the name of Jesus.

59. *For men:* Strengthen our hands, Lord, so that I may not be considered as a thief by my family-in-law. Pay my wife's dowry, in the name of Jesus.

60. *For women:* Strengthen our hands, Lord, so that my husband may not be considered as a thief by my family. Pay my dowry, in the name of Jesus.

61. Spirit of anger, let my husband / my wife go, in the name of Jesus.

62. My home will not stumble by strong drinks or wine, in the name of Jesus.

63. Lord, deliver my husband / my wife from strong drinks, in the name of Jesus.

64. I will not get drunk with wine. I will be filled with the Holy Spirit, in the name of Jesus.

65. How long, Lord, will you let my husband / my wife succumb in drunkenness? Make his wine pass, in the name of Jesus.

66. My husband / my wife, get rid of the mockeries of wine, the tumult of strong drinks, in the name of Jesus.

67. Lord, protect my heart from the rejoicings by wine, in the name of Jesus.

68. *For men:* Power of strong drinks that have absorbed my wife, vomit her, in the name of Jesus.

69. *For women:* Power of strong drinks that have absorbed my husband, vomit him, in the name of Jesus.

70. My feet will not run after strong drinks, in the name of Jesus.

71. I destroy the demonic influences of my family-in-law on my husband / my wife, in the name of Jesus.

72. I scatter by the four winds the meetings held by my family-in-law to use my husband / my wife against me, in the name of Jesus.

73. Any force that made me go away from my parents' house to the matrimonial home, *(choose from the list below)*, be swept by the winds, in the name of Jesus.

    - by abduction, escape, or secrecy
    - by a conspiracy, a plot, or a constraint
    - without the sound of tambourines or harp
    - without the shouts of rejoicing and singing
    - without having kissed my parents

CHAPTER XII

STRANGE THINGS

The final section of this manual deepens the phenomenon of strange things: the moving of objects, the opening and the closing of doors, and finally, the sound of footsteps.

12.1. THE MOVING OF OBJECTS

Joseph, who was a prosperous man, first took the body of Jesus after his death and wrapped it in a clean linen cloth. Then he laid it in a tomb hewn out in the rock. Next he rolled a great stone to the door of the sepulcher and departed (Matthew 27:59-60).

In Matthew 28:1 and 2, it is written,

> In the end of the sabbath, as it began to dawn toward the first day of the week, came Mary Magdalene and the other Mary to see the sepulchre. And, behold, there was a great earthquake: for the angel of the Lord descended from heaven, and came and rolled back the stone from the door, and sat upon it.

At the end of the sabbath, Mary Magdalene and her companion have witnessed an event that took place in the tomb of the Lord Jesus. An angel came down from heaven and rolled the stone, which had been placed by Joseph at the entrance of the tomb and sat on it.

An *angel* is

> a spiritual being superior to humans in power and intelligence; especially: one in the lowest rank in the celestial hierarchy. (*Merriam-Webster Online*, 2013)

Let's analyze the facts of this event of the physical world and of the spiritual world:

- Physical world: The stone rolled at the entrance of the sepulcher has been placed by a human being, thus Joseph. This stone was an object that existed in the physical world.
- Spiritual world: The angel, who operated in the spiritual realm, came from heaven to earth to move the stone that was at the entrance of the tomb. This act confirms the contact between beings of the spiritual world and objects of the physical world.

That is how the stone was rolled away in the absence of a human being, a second time to open the entrance of the tomb.

Now, here is an example of strange things that humans experience. People see, in their homes or elsewhere, tools move without physical assistance. Tools disappear and are found the following days in the same places previously searched. In some cases, these instruments defy the law of gravity and rise from the earth to remain hanging in the air without the assistance of a man. All these activities seem strange to those who do not know the scriptures. Satan's hand is the one that carries out these works through his demons. Whenever such events manifest themselves before you, confront the spirit in the spiritual world that produces these phenomena with the Word, and deliver these objects from the hands of the enemy.

The fact that this angel sat upon the stone he rolled out of the front of the sepulcher proves that spiritual beings can come from other dimensions to sit in your car, bed, living room, balcony, etc. Beloved, it's too dangerous for a Christian who wants to talk to his Heavenly Father to place an empty chair in front of him and ask the Lord Jesus to come and sit there. After that, the person will start to talk to an empty chair by faith, thinking that Christ is sitting there listening to him. This fellow will be surprised if God opens his eyes to let him see that a demon is sitting there, laughing at him. Why does the Lord and Savior have to move from the right hand of the Father, where he is seated, to come and sit on your unholy chair before he can hear you?

12.2. The opening and the closing doors

In this section, the strange phenomenon to study is the opening of doors followed by their closing.

12.2.1. The opening of doors

> And the angel said unto him, Gird thyself, and bind on thy sandals. And so he did. And he saith unto him, Cast thy garment about thee, and follow me. And he went out, and followed him; and wist not

that it was true which was done by the angel; but thought he saw a vision. When they were past the first and the second ward, they came unto the iron gate that leadeth unto the city; which opened to them of his own accord: and they went out, and passed on through one street; and forthwith the angel departed from him. (Acts 12:8-10)

The story began with the imprisonment of Peter by King Herod. At that time, this king abused the church in order to please the Jews. During this same period, the power of God manifested through the apostles. Let us pay attention to verses 8 to 10 in the book of Acts 12 mentioned above:

- In verse eight, the angel asks Peter to come with him.
- In verse nine, Peter leaves the cell and follows the angel. Peter and the angel were in the compartments of the prison. The angel went before Peter, who followed him. The angel was in the spiritual realm, while Peter was in the physical world. It might be that the angel appeared to Peter physically. In this case, we must demonstrate why the presence of the angel was not seen by the guards. (This will be discussed in a forthcoming book on the theme of blindness.)
- In verse 10, we read that the iron gate unlocked by itself. No one exerted physical effort on it.

Likely, Peter witnessed the opening of the iron gate caused by the power of the angel. He was not afraid. Undoubtedly, Peter had no power in him to open the iron gate. He was aware that the angel sent by God to deliver him was walking in front of him and that the door opened only through the power possessed by that angel. Meanwhile, some see the doors of their houses open suddenly, without any human presence, although they live alone. Others find that the refrigerator, the door of the stove, and the faucet are open.

Beloved, why would God open the cupboards or the drawers of your room during your absence? In case you are living similar occurrences, stay firm. Remember that Peter stood before the iron gate when it was unblocked. Did he fled or panicked? All these manifestations indicate the action of evil spirits that are in place to do this variety of activities. When you experience such disturbance, consult the scriptures that expose this matter. Afterward, confront the spirits responsible in prayer. The spirit of the Lord will put them to flight.

There are also people who possess powers that allow them to open doors without touching them. They only need to be placed in front of this door, and it will be open. The power in the spiritual world that precedes them will be the one doing the job. Put your trust in God, and you will see your doors protected from such strange activities.

12.2.2. The closing of doors

> And they that went in, went in male and female of
> all flesh, as God had commanded him: and the Lord
> shut him in. (Genesis 7:16)

After Noah had finished building the ark according to the counsels of God, his family and the animals went on board to escape from the flood. The Lord had planned to exterminate man from the face of the earth that he had created by flooding it with rain for forty days and forty nights. Once inside the ark, the patriarch left the door open. It is the Lord who took care of it for him. That is why the Bible says, "And the Lord shut him in" (Genesis 7:16b). A French version of the Bible (LSG), states in the same verse: "Puis l'Éternel ferma la porte sur lui." All those who were with Noah saw the doors lock without human physical strength. Nobody panicked because they knew that it was an act of God.

After that, the phenomenon of closing doors by spiritual creatures began. Since then, Satan and his demons use this tactic to harm human life. Houses were abandoned by their occupants following this type of event. People can hear the doors of rooms, closets, or showers close by themselves. Once closed, some of the doors do not open despite the efforts made.

Moreover, Noah could not open the door of the ark the Lord had closed. When he wanted to exit, he removed the roof (Genesis 8:13). Beloved, are you embarrassed by such phenomena in your home to the point where you do not know what to do? The right hand of the Lord will free you of this obscure work. Demons have the ability to close a door, a window, a water tap, etc. These evil spirits have the power to keep them stuck without it being possible to reopen them, except through prayer. These strange things should in no way create panic among those who go through them as they are a copy of what the Lord did. Those attacked in this way by Satan should rise in aggressive prayer and confront the invaders of their homes. These evil occupants will be forced to obey the orders you give them, as shown in Psalm 18: 44 and 45:

> As soon as they hear of me, they shall obey me: the strangers shall submit themselves unto me. The strangers shall fade away, and be afraid out of their close places.

12.3. The sound of footsteps

When the Philistines heard that David was anointed king over Israel, they went looking for him. The Lord delivered them into the hand of David, who smote them, on their backs as well as on their stomachs. The Philistines rose once more against the children of Israel. David inquired of the Lord, who made him know his divine plans against his enemies. Let us read what is stated in the Bible:

> As soon as you hear the sound of marching in the tops of the poplar trees, move quickly, because that will mean the Lord has gone out in front of you to strike the Philistine army. (2 Samuel 5:24, NIV)

The Lord told the king to attack the Philistines when he would hear the sounds of marching on the top of the poplar trees. The word *march* means

> To move along steadily usually with a rhythmic stride and in step with others. (*Merriam-Webster Online*, 2013)

The king and his troops camped, awaiting the signal. David was the only one in combat who had the ability to hear the footsteps of the Lord. In Exodus 33, the Lord spoke to Moses:

> For there shall no man see me, and live. (Exodus 33:20b)

Through these scriptures, we understand that the Lord appeared in the tops of the poplar trees with a spiritual body, not a physical body. By using a spiritual body, God moved in front of the army of Israel throughout the battle. The contact of the feet of the Lord with the battlefield produced noise while moving. It is the same for the feet of unclean spirits in houses.

Some people hear in their home or in the surrounding area the sounds of the footsteps of unclean spirits. Troubled by these events, they do not know what to do against this problem, and they choose to move. However, after a while, the same noises are heard in their new home. Sometimes all members of the same family discern the footsteps in the house. Other times, there is only one family member who hears them, while others do not perceive them.

This reminds me of the story of a sister in 2005. In the past, this lady and I had a great discussion on the Christian religion. Her ideas were hostile to the doctrine of spiritual warfare. Sometime later, she called me and told me how she was confronted by footsteps that were heard in the new home she and her husband had just bought. At that time, because I did not know what to do, I brought her to my pastor. He went to pray in her home with strong prayers of deliverance, and the footsteps stopped. The lady then engaged in spiritual warfare and became a member of the body of Christ.

To come back to our teaching, these powers roam into homes and even on the beds of their victims. People attacked by these forces will feel feet that walk on the surface of their bed without seeing them with the naked eye. Beloved, when such situations are found in one place, it shows that demons have already occupied the territory. These spiritual beings must be expelled the way that the Lord Jesus did so in the temple (John 2:14-16).

In the second book of Kings, we read,

> Is not the sound of his master's feet behind him?
> (2 Kings 6:32c)

The king of Israel sent a *messenger* to assassinate the prophet Elisha. He followed the messenger to ensure that the prophet would be executed. But the Lord informed the prophet before the coming of the executioner. Along the way, the Lord God opened the ears of the prophet for him to hear the footsteps of the king hurrying behind his servant. Before the arrival of his murderers, Elisha took measures to prevent the assassination planned against his life.

Two activities of the kingdom of darkness are expressed in the text. First, Satan can inform his servants of the arrival of a visitor by making him perceive in his ears the footsteps of this person. Secondly, Satan can attack a person by making him hear the sounds of footsteps behind him when he is walking or standing. Some people hear footsteps as if human beings were walking behind them. These sounds of footsteps come from the spiritual world and mean that the demons are pursuing them.

Beloved, the adage goes that anyone who makes use of the sword shall perish by the sword. This saying means that the one who is behaving violently shall be victim of the violence. The devil has launched his fiery darts against you. Now it is time to return them to him. The prayers that are presented at the end of this chapter will help you rule over these abnormal things that expose themselves around you.

12.4. PRAYER SECTION

1. I cast out the strange things that manifest themselves in my life, in my family, and in my home, in the name of Jesus.
2. I frustrate the fear that I have from strange things, in the name of Jesus.
3. My eyes will not see strange things, in the name of Jesus.
4. I condemn the strange things that occur in this environment, in the name of Jesus.
5. Lord, drop stones on the evil angels who left heaven to move objects in this house, in the name of Jesus.
6. Lord, drop hailstones on the evil spirit that left the waters or the mountains to levitate objects in this house, in the name of Jesus.
7. I bring down to the grave the spirits that make objects walk in this house, in the name of Jesus.
8. Evil spirit sitting on an object in this house, come down and sit in the dust, in the name of Jesus.
9. Hands of the powers of darkness laid on the tools in this house, dry off, in the name of Jesus.
10. Utensils of this house will be burning coals in the hands of evil spirits, in the name of Jesus.
11. By the blood of Jesus, I abolish the contact between objects in this house and occult powers, in the name of Jesus.
12. Angel of Satan placed in front of the door of this house, be devoured by famine, in the name of Jesus.
13. The doors of this house will not open in the presence of evil spirits, in the name of Jesus.
14. I exterminate the powers that give men the ability to open doors without touching them, in the name of Jesus.
15. Lord, destroy the quivering and noise produced by the arrival of the spirits that come to roll objects in this house, in the name of Jesus.

16. Evil wind blown by malignant spirits in order to open the doors of this house, go back into their mouths, in the name of Jesus.

17. Mighty One of Jacob, open the iron gates placed in front of my destiny, before my career, and those placed at the entrance of my promised land and my blessings, in the name of Jesus.

18. Holy Ghost, put to flight the evil spirits who walk in front of me and the powers that go before my enemies, in the name of Jesus.

19. Spirit of God, put to flight the forces that come to open the windows, the faucets, the cabinets, the stoves, the curtains, the pots, the refrigerators, and the freezers of this house, in the name of Jesus.

20. Any demon that closes the doors of this house, be precipitated into everlasting fire, in the name of Jesus.

21. Lord, do violence to the hands of evil angels stretched to close the doors of this house, in the name of Jesus.

22. Any door in this house and in my life that are closed by evil spirits, be released from their grip, in the name of Jesus.

23. I nail in the ground the feet of the evil forces that walk in this place, in the name of Jesus.

24. I command the feet of the forces walking in this place to be chained by fire, in the name of Jesus.

25. Any demon who makes the noise of his footsteps in this place to be heard, lose your power, in the name of Jesus.

26. My ears, reject the sounds of the footsteps of evil spirits, in the name of Jesus.

27. Any demon opening my ears to hear the sounds of the footsteps of the spiritual world, I throw feces on your face, in the name of Jesus.

28. By the blood of Jesus, I draw a limit to the footsteps of the spirits in the spiritual world, in the name of Jesus.

29. Angel of the Lord, trouble the sounds of the footsteps of the spirits that are being heard behind me, in the name of Jesus.

30. Angel of the Lord, trouble the sounds of the footsteps of the powers that are being heard in front of me, in the name of Jesus.

31. Let the footsteps of the spirits that will cross the doors of my house flip over, in the name of Jesus.

32. Let the noises of the footsteps of spiritual forces stagger, in the name of Jesus.

33. O earth, hear the words of my mouth. Fight the forces that make sounds of their footsteps behind me, in the name of Jesus.

34. By the power in the blood of Jesus, I erase my footprints on earth, in the name of Jesus.

35. Lord, consume the footsteps that are heard behind me, in the name of Jesus.

36. Any force of the night walking slowly in this house and resonating

    - the rings of his feet
    - the rod in his hand

    be covered by the waters of the Red Sea, in the name of Jesus.

GLOSSARY

adultery: "Voluntary sexual intercourse between a married man and someone other than his wife or between a married woman and someone other than her husband" (*Merriam-Webster Online*, 2013).

angel: "A spiritual being superior to humans in power and intelligence; especially: one in the lowest rank in the celestial hierarchy" (*Merriam-Webster Online, 2013*).

anger: "A strong feeling of displeasure and usually of antagonism" (*Merriam-Webster Online*, 2013).

attraction: "A force acting mutually between particles of matter, tending to draw them together, and resisting their separation" *(Merriam-Webster Online*, 2013).

beauty: "1) The quality or aggregate of qualities in a person or thing that gives pleasure to the senses or pleasurably exalts the mind or spirit: loveliness; 2) A beautiful person or thing; especially: a beautiful woman" (*Merriam-Webster Online*, 2013).

blast: "A violent gust of wind" (*Merriam-Webster Online*, 2013).

chief: "Accorded highest rank or office" (*Merriam-Webster Online*, 2013).

catch up: "To travel fast enough to overtake an advance party" (*Merriam-Webster Online*, 2013).

deliverance: "The state of being saved from something dangerous or unpleasant. Liberation, rescue" (*Merriam-Webster Online*, 2013).

demon: "An evil spirit" (*Merriam-Webster Online*, 2013).

deity: "The rank or essential nature of a god: divinity" (Merriam-Webster Online, 2013).

dream: "A series of thoughts, images, or emotions occurring during sleep and especially during rapid eye movement (REM) sleep" (*Merriam-Webster Online*, 2013).

false prophet: "A prophet who is not a member of a new creation priesthood of Jesus Christ, one who prophesies and performs prophetic functions on behalf of the devil, even if in the flesh" (*The Prophet's Dictionary, The Ultimate Guide to Supernatural Wisdom*, p. 207).

flesh: "1) The soft parts of the body of an animal and especially of a vertebrate; especially: the parts composed chiefly of skeletal muscle as distinguished from internal organs, bone, and integument; 2) The physical nature of human beings" (*Merriam-Webster Online*, 2013).

flying: "Moving or capable of moving in the air" (*Merriam-Webster Online*, 2013).

gust: "1) A sudden brief rush of wind; 2) A sudden outburst: surge" (*Merriam-Webster Online*, 2013).

harlot: "Prostitute" (*Merriam-Webster Online*, 2013).

holocaust: "A sacrifice consumed by fire" (*Merriam-Webster Online*, 2013).

kind: "1) Affectionate, loving; 2) Of a sympathetic or helpful nature; 3) Of a forbearing nature: gentle" (*Merriam-Webster Online*, 2013).

kindness: "1) A kind deed: favor; 2) Archaic: affection" (*Merriam-Webster Online*, 2013).

lift: "To raise from a lower to a higher position: elevate" (*Merriam-Webster Online*, 2013).

majesty: "1) Sovereign power, authority, or dignity; 2) Greatness or splendor of quality or character" (*Merriam-Webster Online*, 2013).

mantle: "A loose sleeveless garment worn over other clothes: cloak" (*Merriam-Webster Online*, 2013).

messenger: "One who bears a message or does an errand" *(Merriam-Webster Online, 2013).*

niter: "Potassium nitrate" *(Merriam-Webster Online, 2013).*

nitre: "Niter" (*Merriam-Webster Online*, 2013).

nose: "1) The part of the face that bears the nostrils and covers the anterior part of the nasal cavity; broadly: this part together with the nasal cavity; 2) The sense of smell; 3) The vertebrate olfactory organ" (*Merriam-Webster Online*, 2013).

offering: "Something offered; especially: a sacrifice ceremonially offered as a part of worship" (*Merriam-Webster Online*, 2013).

potassium nitrate: "A crystalline salt KNO_3 that is a strong oxidizing agent and is used in medicine chiefly as a diuretic—called also niter, saltpeter" (*Merriam-Webster Online*, 2013).

prophet: "Person who speaks by divine inspiration, revealing or interpreting the will of a god" (*Merriam-Webster Online*, 2013).

prostitute: "1) A woman who engages in promiscuous sexual intercourse especially for money: whore; 2) A male who engages in sexual and especially homosexual practices for money" (*Merriam-Webster Online*, 2013).

ride: "1) To sit and travel on the back of an animal that one directs; 2) To travel as if on a conveyance: be borne; 3) To move like a floating object."

sacrifice: "An act of offering to a deity something precious; especially: the killing of a victim on an altar" (*Merriam-Webster Online*, 2013).

smell: "1) To perceive the odor or scent of through stimuli affecting the olfactory nerves: get the odor or scent of with the nose. 2) To detect or become aware of as if by the sense of smell" (*Merriam-Webster Online*, 2013).

strange gods: "Mentioned in the King James Version of the bible no less than eleven times, the word refers to false gods. Prophetic function on behalf of the devil, even if in the flesh" (Price 2006, p. 543).

tabernacle: "1) A often capitalized: a tent sanctuary used by the Israelites during the Exodus; 2) Archaic: a dwelling place; 3) Archaic: a temporary shelter: tent" (*Merriam-Webster Online*, 2013).

theraphim: "A) Images. A household god thought to guard and guide the home and its family affairs. B) Usually a statue or a figurine. Judges 17:5 and 18:4, 17-18; Hosea 3:4" (Price 2006, p. 555).

tradition: "1) An inherited, established, or customary pattern of thought, action, or behavior (as a religious practice or a social custom); 2) A belief or story or a body of beliefs or stories relating to the past that are commonly accepted as historical though not verifiable" (*Merriam-Webster Online*, 2013).

turn: "1) To cause to move around an axis or a center: make rotate or revolve; 2) To bend or change the course of" (*Merriam-Webster Online*, 2013).

twist: "1) To alter the meaning of; 2) To pull off, turn, or break by torsion" (*Merriam-Webster Online*, 2013).

REFERENCES

Holy Bible, New International Version®, © 1973, 1978, 1984, 2011 by Biblica, Inc. ® Used by permission. All rights reserved worldwide.

Holy Bible. New King James Version, © 1982 by Thomas Nelson, Inc.

La Bible. Version Louis Second.

Merriam-Webster Online (2013). www.merriam-webster.com/ Merriam-Webster, Incorporated, consulted in April 2013

Price, Paula, PhD. 2006. *The Prophet's Dictionary: The Ultimate Guide to Supernatural Wisdom.* Whitaker House: New Kensington, PA.